Shelter *from the* Storm

FACILITATOR'S GUIDE

Hope for Survivors of Sexual Abuse

Facilitator's Guide by
Jacqualine C. Truitt

Lifeway Pre
Nashvi lle,Tennessee

ACKNOWLEDGEMENTS

Shelter from the Storm: Hope for Survivors of Sexual Abuse Facilitator's Guide
Copyright ©1995 LifeWay Press

LifeWay Press books are published by The Sunday School Board, 127 Ninth Avenue, North, Nashville, Tennessee 37234

For help for facilitators and leaders in carrying out LIFE® Support Group Series ministries in your church, call 1-615-251-5613.

Item 7209-44
ISB   0-8054-9980-6
Dewey Decimal Number 362.88
Subject Heading: SEX CRIMES // VICTIMS OF CRIME

Unless otherwise indicated, biblical quotations are from the Holy Bible, *New International Version,* copyright © 1973, 1978, 1984 by International Bible Society (NIV). Other versions used: the *New American Standard Bible* (NASB) ©The Lockman Foundation, 1960, 1962, 1963, 1968, 1971, 1972, 1973, 1975, 1977. Used by permission; the *King fames Version* (KJV).

Printed in the United States of America

Contents

THE AUTHOR

 Jacqualine C. Truitt is a licensed professional counselor, a licensed family therapist, and a certified trauma resolution therapist. She owns and operates the NewLife Counseling Center, Pasadena, Texas

LIFE® Support Group Series **Editorial Team**
Dale McCleskey, Editor
Kenny Adams, Manuscript Assistant

David Walley, Team Leader/LIFE® Support Group Series Specialist

Graphics by Lori Putnam
Cover Design by Edward Crawford

Introduction

People in churches are asking, "Why should the local church become involved in the support and recovery ministry?" We have a responsibility to God to ask that question about any ministry. We must also ask, "Is God working in this ministry and is He revealing Himself through His work?"

As more and more people share their deepest hurts and pains, they are asking, "Can and will God respond to my need?" They are asking similar questions about the church. "Does the church care about my pain?"

The Gospels are filled with examples of Jesus meeting the needs of people-examples of His response to the broken-hearted, the emotionally and physically needy, and the diseased. It saddens me to hear Christian friends say that they cannot share their hurts and pains with their friends at church. As a counselor I often hear: "I can't tell my Christian friends that I was sexually abused or raped. I can't tell them that my father was an alcoholic and that his alcoholism is still affecting my life. When I try to talk about it they tell me that if I had enough faith none of that would bother me anymore. But it does bother me and I feel like such a failure. I want my friends to like me so I just fake it and pretend that everything is fine."

The Bible clearly teaches us to "bear one another's burdens and thus fulfill the law of Christ" (Galatians 6:2, NASB). Christians experience physical, psychological, spiritual, and emotional pain as a part of the human condition. In Luke 4:18-19, KJV, Jesus said, "The Spirit of the Lord is upon me, because he hath anointed me to preach the gospel to the poor; he hath sent me to heal the brokenhearted, to preach deliverance to the captives, and recovering of sight to the blind, to set at liberty them that are bruised, to preach the acceptable year of the Lord."

If the church is actively to be the body of Christ, then the church must minister as Christ ministered-to the total person. Jesus said: "I was hungry and you gave me food, I was in prison and you visited me, I was thirsty and you gave me drink. Whatsoever you have done to the least of these you have done unto me." The reason for and heartbeat of a Christ-centered recovery ministry in the local church is a biblical mandate. John records that mandate in John 17:18. Jesus said, "As you (the Heavenly Father) sent me into the world, I have sent them into the world."

Shelter from the Storm is a resource for adult survivors of sexual abuse. It is designed to help the individual come face-to-face with life's traumatic issues. Participants need to understand that Shelter groups are not therapy groups but Christ-centered caring and sharing groups that help people deal with the issues related to their experience of sexual abuse. *Shelter from the Storm* is a part of the LIFE® Support Group Series of resources.

What is the LIFE® Support Group Series?

The LIFE® Support Group Series is an educational system of discovery-group and support-group resources providing Christian ministry and emotional support of individuals in areas of spiritual social, emotional, and physical need.

A discovery group studies resources on dysfunctional-family issues and other problem areas individuals face. A group leader guides group discussion of the content and helps group members consider applications to their lives. Members of discovery groups will explore personal issues and emotions, but the primary focus of the group is discussing the content in the member's book. These discovery groups generally are less emotionally intense. A caring, sensitive group leader without specialized skills or training can lead them.

Because discovery groups are less intense, they provide excellent starting points for churches launching support-group ministries. *Search for Significance*, LIFE® Support Group Series Edition, *Untangling Relationships: A Christian Perspective on Codependency* , and *Breaking the Cycle of Hurtful Family Experiences* are discovery group resources.

A support group is more focused than a discovery group and is composed of people who meet because of personal issues common to group members . A support group focuses on helping members gain awareness; understanding; and emotional, psychological, and spiritual support for dealing with personal-life issues. While a discovery group meets to learn about a painful life issue, a support group is a group of people who all share that life issue. Support groups meet not so much to learn about but to change the pattern of thoughts, feelings, and behaviors. *Shelter from the Storm* is a support group because those joining the group share a common issue--sexual abuse.

LIFE® Support Group Series resources provide help for three types of support groups:

1. Encouragement and Accountability Support Group. Members encourage and support each other's progress toward a goal. A discovery-group level of leadership skills is sufficient for this type of support group. *First Place: A Christ-Centered Health Program*, which helps adults improve their mental, physical, and emotional health under Christ's lordship, and *Quitting for Good, A Christ-Centered Approach to Nicotine Dependency* are resources for this type of support group.

2. Personal-Issues Support Group. Members share personal responses to issues and problems with which they are dealing. The group provid"es a safe and loving environment for personal and spiritual healing , growth, and recovery. *Making Peace with Your Past, Moving Beyond Your Past*, and *A Time for Healing: Coming to Terms with Your Divorce* are resources for this type of support group. Such groups need a skilled lay facilitator because of the volatile emotions that may erupt in group sessions. *Shelter from the Storm: Hope for Survivors of Sexual Abuse* is a personal issues support group study.

3. 12-Step Support Group. Members use a Christ-centered 12-Step program to help each other make progress in recover y from addictions. The process includes repentance, trust in God, and spiritual renewal. Twelve-Step support groups also require a skilled lay facilitator to guide the group sessions.

Resources for Christ-centered 12-Step support groups include *Conquering Codependency: A Christ-Centered 12-Step Process; Conquering Eating Disorders: A Christ-Centered 12-Step Process; Conquering Chemical Dependenel: A Christ-Centered 12-Step Process;* and *Conquering Chemical Dependency: First Steps to a Christ-Centered 12-Step Process.*

Facilitating a Support Group

Facilitating a support group is not the same as leading a Bible study or teaching a lesson. Special skills are necessary to handle the situations that can arise in the group sessions. Do not attempt to lead a *Shelter* group until you have adequate training and the skills to do so. You are preparing for one of the most challenging and gratifying experiences in life-lead ing a sexual abuse support group. Throughout church history, God has used small groups to strengthen and motivate people. The support and encouragement found within the group provides an environment where people can be more vulnerable about their weaknesses and more

open to both believing and applying the truth of God's Word. Facilitating a group like this serves the members and gives honor to the Lord.

If you meet the criteria, the following material will help you prepare for your support group. Complete the steps recommended for starting a group and carefully study the material provided in this guide. Make prayer a major part of your preparation. Seek God's help throughout this process and give glory to Him for all of the progress that will take place in participants' lives.

Note: Page numbers identified in this facilitator's guide will be preceded by "FG." All other page references refer to pages in the member's book.

Goals for a *Shelter from the Storm* Support Group

1. Offer caring support and encouragement. *Shelter* groups are not therapy groups. They are Christ-centered support groups. People who have experienced the pain of sexual abuse usually carry that pain alone for many years. They need to feel the support and encouragement of others so they can face the pain of the abuse and experience healing.

2. Offer unconditional love and acceptance. Survivors of sexual abuse feel illegitimate shame and guilt regardless of the circumstances of the abuse. As survivors talk about the experience in an atmosphere of unconditional love and acceptance, they begin to accept their own thoughts and feelings. They also begin to accept themselves.

3. Offer a safe and trusted place for wounded people to tell the truth. Survivors of sexual abuse typically are not aware of how dishonest they have been with themselves and with others about the abuse. They often minimize, rationalize, or make excuses to avoid the pain of the abuse or the loss of the idealized image of the perpetrator or family. A strong feeling among survivors is: "If you knew what happened to me and how dirty I feel inside you could not love me or accept me." Survivors need a safe place to begin to tell themselves the truth about the sexual abuse.

4. Offer an environment to express feelings openly. Survivors of sexual abuse often experience what is called "Post-traumatic Stress Disorder" or PTSD. One of the symptoms of PTSD is the numbing of feelings. In the safety of a *Shelter* group, survivors begin to experience, communicate, and label feelings, sometimes for the first time in their lives. Many survivors were abused by members of their families or grew up in otherwise dysfunctional families. Among the many rules of dysfunctional families is the spoken or unspoken rule that says, "Don't feel." If you happen to recognize a feeling, a second rule moves into place and gives the instruction "don't talk about it." A *Shelter* group is a healthy family that encourages the survivor to express feelings openly.

5. Offer freedom to identify options and make decisions. Survivors must make many decisions as they progress through the recovery process. These include decisions such as whom to tell about the abuse, whether to take legal action against the perpetrator, and whether to confront the perpetrator. The symp-toms of sexual abuse also affect decisions about marriage, friendships, and career.

6. Offer a safe place to take the time needed to recover. Friends and family members often tire of the process long before the survivor has worked through the pain and grief of recovery. Those who have not experienced the impact of abuse have a difficult time understanding the effects or the time required to heal. *Shelter* group members will understand and encourage other members to take the time they need to recover.

7. Offer an opportunity to expose hurtful experiences and unmet needs without being misunderstood and criticize?. Friends and family members often unknow-ingly make painful statements to the survivor regarding the abuse. In a *Shelter* group, you will guide your group members through these painful statement s. Group members will discover painful insights into their issues. As a group facilitator, you need to support these members without rescuing them.

8. Offer a place to experience accountability to yourself and to others. Group members are accountable for: attendance and participation in the group, maintaining confidentiality and personal honesty, for openness with other group members, and for working on their issues. In the process of group life, the members learn or rediscover how to experience life with others in a real and meaningful way.

9. Offer an experience of the mercy and wisdom of God and the healing power of prayer. As group members share their own experience with God, others in the group begin to realize that God has been merciful to them. They too can seek wisdom from Him and experience the healing power of an active prayer life.

10. Offer hope and healing. Victims of sexual abuse feel hopeless until they see that someone else has faced the reality of the abuse and found healing. As you and other members of the group model healing, they slowly begin to believe that they too can recover.

11. Offer community to those who have felt alone in their grief and pain. Victims live in a world of silence. They hold the grief and pain of the abuse deep inside, surrounded by layers of protection. To be close to others threatens them. A *Shelter* group provides the fellowship of suffering-the fellowship of Jesus.

Facilitator Qualifications

A *Shelter from the Storm* group can be led by either a professional counselor or a trained layperson. Groups that are counselor facilitated and those facilitated by a layperson each have their own advantages and disadvantages. I recommend that a trained Christian counselor lead the group, but if your church cannot acquire the services of a counselor, the following suggestions may help you to prepare to meet the needs of your group in a safe and competent manner.

Read this facilitator's guide and the member's book, *Shelter from the Storm: Hope and Healing for Survivors of Sexual Abuse.* Establish a clear understanding of your goals for the group by reading the goals in this guide and adding any others you believe to be important. Reading these materials will familiarize you with the course content and help you feel more confident in your role as a facilitator.

A facilitator for a *Shelter from the Storm* group who is a licensed counselor should:

1. State clearly that a *Shelter* group is a support group, not a therapy group. The facilitator must not function as a counselor. One of the disadvantages of a counselor-facilitated group is the tendency of th counselor to move into a therapeutic role. The grou covenant must clearly state that this is a suppo group, not a therapy group. The facilitator must con mit to maintain a support group format.

One of the differences between a therapy group and support group is that in a support group the facilitate is expected to be significantly self-disclosing. A cou selor should have experience in a support group fo mat before facilitating a *Shelter* group.

2. Establish a personal support system while facil tating the group. Counselors are highly trained ind vidual who are used to dealing with other people problems; however, I encourage everyone who facil tates a *Shelter* group to be willing to establish a pe sonal support system. The intensity of the issues th. arise in a sexual abuse group can be overwhelming. facilitator needs to establish and maintain a solid cli ical and spiritual support base for personal protectic as well as for the protection of the group.

A facilitator for a *Shelter from the Storm* group who is *not* licensed as a counselor should:

1. Be supervised by a professional counselor or pa toral counselor familiar with sexual abuse issue Even the most skilled facilitator may become ove whelmed by the intensity of the issues within a sexu abuse support group. A facilitator needs to establi and maintain both a clinical and a spiritual suppo base for personal protection as well as for the prote tion of the group.

2. Establish a personal support system while faci tating the group. The intensity of the issues that ari in a sexual abuse group can be overwhelming. A fac itator needs to establish and maintain a solid clinic and spiritual support base for personal protection well as for the protection of the group.

3. Be willing to address personal issues in a suppc group format before attempting to facilitate a sexu abuse support group. If the facilitator is a survivor sexual abuse, he will need to have experienced signi cant recovery prior to facilitating the group. Part that recovery journey should be in a support gro setting. If the facilitator is not a survivor of sexu

abuse, she should participate in a *Making Peace with Your Past* group before attempting to facilitate a *Shelter from the Storm* Group.

4. Be willing to invest considerable time and energy to learn about sexual abuse. Becoming an effective facilitator is an ongoing process. Read books on sexual-abuse recovery, take advantage of training opportunities, and listen to your group members.

Essential Qualifications:

Any person-lay or professional-seeking to facilitate a *Shelter from the Storm* group needs to first serve as an apprentice co-facilitator in a support group before they facilitate a *Shelter* group. In addition, they must possess the following basic qualities that are necessary for any group facilitator.

A facilitator should:

1. Be a growing Christian, a person of prayer, and a person who has faith in what God can do.
2. Possess Christian values.
3. Have a knowledge of the process of recovery from sexual abuse.
4. Sense God's call to be involved in ministry.
5. Be spiritually gifted for the work.
6. Be an active member of a local church.
7. Relate well to people.
8. Have a commitment to keep confidential information private.
9. Be willing to give time and energy to help group members.
10. Have a teachable spirit.
11. Be personally involved in the recovery process.
12. Be emotionally stable.[1]

Before taking the responsibility of being a facilitator for a sexual abuse support group, ask yourself the following questions:

1. Am I emotionally, psychologically, and physically prepared to deal with the potentially intense and volatile emotions that will emerge within the group?
2. Do I have a clear understanding of my motivation for wanting to lead a *Shelter from the Storm* group?
3. If you are a survivor-Am I far enough into my own recovery to manage my own issues without them becoming the focus of the group?
4. If you are not a survivor-Do I understand sexual abuse issues well enough to empathize with the group members?
5. Am I willing to allow the group to confront me about my own recovery issues?

Facilitators of *Shelter from the Storm* support groups need to have demonstrated a commitment to their own spiritual and relational development. This can be done by participating in other LIFE ® and LIFE ® Support Group Series groups.

LIFE® Courses such as *MasterLife,* Disciple's *PrayerLife,* and *Experiencing God* can help provide the spiritual foundation for leading a *Shelter* group. Facilitators will benefit greatly from a thorough understanding of *WiseCounsel: Skills for Lay Counseling.*

LIFE® Support Group Series courses such as *Search for Significance* LIFE ® Support Group Series Edition , *Untangling Relationships, Conquering Codependency, Making Peace with Your Past,* and *Moving Beyond Your Past* can help provide the relational development needed to facilitate a *Shelter* group.

Notes

1Tim Sledge, *Making Peace with Your Past Facilitator's Guide,* (Nashville: LifeWay Press, 1992), p. 5.

Taking Care of the Facilitator

Facilitating a *Shelter* group can be a very gratifying experience, but it can also be a very trying experience. You will need to take care of yourself. No one can withstand the impact of hearing multiple stories of intense anguish and pain without support. As suggested under "Facilitator Qualifications," you will need a method for resolving your own issues which arise as a result of the stories you hear and the lives you touch.

You will find many people who do not understand the devastation of sexual abuse. They do not understand the time required to heal from the damaging effects. These people tend to be unsupportive because of their lack of understanding.

Burnout

If you do not take care of yourself, you will experience burnout. Prepare yourself. Become familiar with the following symptoms of burnout.
- A generalized feeling of anger
- Helplessness
- Hopelessness
- A feeling of ineffectiveness
- A growing sense of disillusionment with the human condition
- Depression
- Apathy
- A feeling of dread as group time approaches
- A knot in your stomach when the phone rings
- A desire to run away

To avoid burnout, make a conscious decision to take each of the following actions:

1. Do not be the caretaker for the group or for any individual in the group.

   The first unit in *Shelter from the Storm: Hope and Healing for Survivors of Sexual Abuse* will help you with this problem. Each group member is to designate a list of resource people. Be persistent in requiring that this list be completed within the first two weeks after an individual joins the group.

2. Do not try to be the therapist for the group or for any individual in the group.

A difference exists between a therapist and a support group facilitator. Your role is to facilitate the group process. The therapist interprets and investigates. Resist the urge to practice therapy.

3. Find an outlet for your own feelings as you facilitate this group.

The best possible solution to the isolation many support group facilitators experience is to be involved in individual or group therapy. If this is not available, find someone to meet with you on a regular basis who has led a support group or has been a member of a group. The need for contact with someone of significant understanding and experience with recovery is important. If your pastor, another staff member, or small-group coordinator understands support and recovery, schedule a regular time to talk with this individual. Do not attempt to facilitate a *Shelter* group without your own support system in place before you start.

4. Involve yourself with other people who are not survivors of sexual abuse.

No matter how intensely you feel a burden for survivors of sexual abuse, spend time focusing on other issues. You need a continuous reminder that some people do not harm and exploit others and that not everyone has suffered the exploitation of sexual abuse.

5. Take a break occasionally.

Occasionally the facilitator needs to take a break. A co-facilitator or a licensed counselor can step in to lead the group. Recognize when you need a break and take it.

Understanding Group Life

Your task as a facilitator is to create a safe atmosphere in which members can talk about their sexual abuse issues. As you prepare to facilitate a group, you need to evaluate your expectations and responsibilities.

Expectations

What do you expect group members to learn and do as a result of participating in this study? Will they become great theologians, live perfect lives, and fulfill the Great Commission as they serve as missionaries in Peru? Thoughts like these may seem ridiculous, yet many of us have misplaced expectations for our group which can lead to frustration and anger.

Our expectations need to coincide with the commitment level of our group members . If they sincerely desire to study and be accountable to one another in applying what they learn, then you can expect exciting things to happen! If, on the other hand, their commitment is only to attend group meetings, you will need to lower your expectations.

Regardless of your group's current commitment level, realize that their motivation may change. God can use your prayers and enthusiasm to impart to others a greater desire to learn and apply truth to their lives.

Three general levels of commitment are usually demonstrated by members of small groups.

1. To attend meetings and observe the proceedings without having done any personal study.
2. To read through the material without answering the questions.
3. To work through the material, writing out answers and applying to their lives the concepts in each lesson.

The third level is by far the most effective. Even if the group members begin at the first or second level of commitment, hopefully they will reach the deepest level of commitment as time progresses. This facilitator's guide assumes that members are working at the third level because it asks for responses from the work for each unit.

All groups are not created equal. A group of people who are initially strangers to one another will require different leadership than a group of friends who know each other very well. Since the members of a *Shelter* group probably never have met as a group for this purpose before, they will probably go through all of the stages of group development described below.

Stages of a Group

Groups develop their own personality and seem to have a life of their own. Each group you facilitate will be different . Additionally, each group will change while you are facilitating it.

Groups seem to go through three identifiable stages. The issues, feelings, and actions of group members will change as your group moves through these stages.

In the three stages, group members deal with–
- First stage: issues
- Second stage: feelings
- Third stage: actions

In stage one, members experience, feel, and act on a sense of–
- belonging
- excitement
- superficial communication
- safety or security
- nervousness
- fear
- little self-disclosure
- caution
- the development of group identity
- anticipation

In stage two, members begin to do or to display the following-
- increasing trust
- a questioning attitude
- less excitement
- some drop out
- more self-determined goals
- a sense of purpose
- impatience
- anxiety
- disclosure
- some finally begin to emotionally join the group
- frustration
- group goals
- more willingness to be vulnerable

11

In stage three, members may be described by-
- goal-oriented behavior
- feeling of acceptance and encouragement
- greater commitment to the group
- commitment to the task
- freedom
- determination
- greater commitment to each other
- connected
- willing to allow and work through conflict
- reaching out to other group members
- beginning to share leadership

Responsibility

Each person is responsible to be actively involved in the group. Group members demonstrate responsibility by two actions; they tune in, and they talk up.

Group life requires that each person actively participate by tuning in to the issues of others and talking about their own issues. Survivors tend to act in one of two extremes: They tune out and shut up, or they display hostility and anger. Your group will not survive if you allow members to tune out and avoid talking. You will also face challenges dealing with members' anger.

Each group member can tune in by:
- listening to what others are saying;
- paying attention to their own feelings and reactions when someone else is communicating;
- being sensitive to the feelings others expressed verbally and nonverbally.

Each group member can talk up by:
- giving appropriate and constructive feedback;
- checking out their perception of what others say or mean;
- sharing their reaction to what others have shared;
- being responsible for their own recovery.

The group is not responsible for the recovery of the individual. Each person must take responsibility for his or her own needs.

Confidentiality

Confidentiality includes who is in the group as well as what is said in the group. Group members must learn never to disclose what is said in the group, and they must never disclose the identities of group members.

All of us need to feel secure, but this is especially true of those who have been victims of sexual abuse. As sexual abuse victims begin to recover and are able to participate in group activities, privacy becomes a key factor.

Maintaining confidentiality builds an atmosphere of trust and security. Emphasize to the group the need for privacy. The names and situations of group members should not be discussed outside the group. Mention of any group member's attendance to anyone other than a group member or a counselor must be prohibited.

The facilitator should make it clear that members do not have to give telephone numbers, even for a class list. Each member needs to understand that he or she has these freedoms. Every member needs to have confidence that no one will violate the agreement made in the group not to discuss the members or the meetings outside tl;le group.

Trust is 'an essential part of group life. As the group members share facts about themselves in the form of details of the abuse, thought patterns, feelings and behaviors that are the consequences of the abuse, it is important to have confidence that those facts will not be shared outside of the group.

Respecting Physical Boundaries

Learning to express appropriate forms of intimacy is an important part of group life. Appropriate intimacy includes such issues as learning to talk about sensitive subjects without totally exposing our thoughts and feelings. We learn that we can freely choose whether and to what degree to be emotionally intimate. In the same way, we learn to establish healthy physical boundaries. We learn that we can choose to give and receive physical expressions of love and support, or we can choose not to give or receive physical touch. We can develop the ability to give and receive an affirming, non-sexual hug, but we must respect each other's boundaries. No one should hug or touch another member without first asking permission.

Steps for Starting a *Shelter* Support Group

Shelter from the Storm: Hope and Healing for Survivors of Sexual Abuse can be used in one of several different formats to meet your needs as a facilitator and the needs of your group. The following steps will guide you through the process of establishing a *Shelter from the Storm* group. If a church leader has enlisted you to facilitate this group, some of the steps may have already been completed.

0 Pray
0 Secure approval
0 Obtain training as a Support Group Facilitator
0 Obtain training for *Shelter from the Storm*
0 Secure a supervisor
0 Establish a referral list
0 Decide on child care
0 Determine a format: set a time, date, and place
0 Order materials
0 Decide on promotional efforts
0 Set fees for materials
0 Get started

The success of your group will depend on your careful planning. Prepare yourself and your church to minister effectively to survivors of sexual abuse.

Step 1: Pray
Prayer is the beginning of any ministry. You have this resource in your hands because God has made you aware of how He cares about survivors of sexual abuse. How does God want you to join Him in His work? You can find that answer as you saturate yourself in Bible study and prayer. When God reveals to you where He is working, it is usually because He is inviting you to join Him. Don't make your own plans and then ask God to bless them. Let your ministry be led by what God is already doing in your midst.

Step 2: Secure Approval
If you believe God is calling you to facilitate a *Shelter from the Storm* group, the next step on your journey is to seek the approval of your pastor or the appropriate staff or lay leader in your church. If your church has a LIFE® Support Group coordinator, contact this person. Schedule a time that will allow a full explanation of your interest in facilitating a *Shelter* group. Bring a copy of this facilitator's guide and the member's book. Review the purpose, content, goals, and procedures for the group. Go over the recommendations for facilitators and respond to any questions. Do not expect the

pastor or church leader to give you an immediate response. Allow time for a review of the material and consideration of the ministry. Remember, this is a sensitive subject. Be prepared for the leader to express some reservations. Do not take the leader's reservations personally. Ask the staff or lay leader to review the materials and pray about the need and possibility of the group and about your preparedness to serve as facilitator of the group. Schedule a time to meet again.

If you are a church staff member, do not strike out on your own without seeking approval and support from other leaders on your staff or in your congregation. Express clearly the fact that this material is part of a Christ-centered discipleship process. Explain that the group will follow guidelines for providing the clinical and emotional support needed for facilitating the group. Even if you are a church staff member, recognize that your education and training may not be sufficient to lead a *Shelter* group. Evaluate your preparedness to facilitate this group and seek training as a support group facilitator and as a *Shelter* facilitator.

Step 3: Obtain Training as Support Group Facilitator
The skills of a facilitator are learned best by experiencing them under the leadership of a skilled support-group facilitator and by practicing them as an apprentice. If you have not learned these skills in a group process, consider one of the following suggestions for developing the necessary skills.

1. Participate as a member of a support group being offered in your church or in another church.
2. Participate in another type of intensive support-group process for a period of time.
3. Attend an intensive training event in which skilled facilitators help you see, develop, and practice support-group-facilitation skills. The Sunday School Board conducts facilitator-training events. To learn about training events call 1-615-251-5613.

Please do not attempt to facilitate a support group without adequate preparation. If you do, members could have an experience that causes more harm than good. The *LIFE Support Leader's Handbook* (Item 7268-02 available by calling 1-800-458-2772 or from your Baptist Book Store or Lifeway Christian Store) will help you prepare for the task of administering a support-group ministry. You may use the *LIFE ® Support Group Series Training Video* (Item 7700-24) to help you train leaders.

I strongly encourage you not to do *Shelter* as your first support group. Begin with a discovery-group course. Then participate or facilitate a personal-issues support group or a 12-Step support group. The need for a *Shelter* group may seem so great that you must hurry, but remember that you will do hurting people no favor by attempting to facilitate a group for which you are unprepared. Sexual abuse survivors will benefit greatly from participation in a discovery group, a *Conquering Codependency* group, or a *Making Peace with Your Past* group. Do yourself and your group members a favor. Go slowly. Prepare well, and you will experience success.

Step 4: Obtain Specific Training to be a *Shelter from the Storm* Group Facilitator

Contact Southern Baptist state or associational leadership or call 1-615-251-5613 about training to facilitate the group. If you have never been in a support group or facilitated a group, participate in another LIFE® Support Group Series group and seek training before beginning a *Shelter from the Storm* group. As you read this facilitator's guide you will realize the need for special skills as a facilitator. You also will realize the intensity of the issues addressed in a *Shelter* group, and you will identify the need for an advanced knowledge of sexual abuse.

Step 5: Secure a Supervisor

A *Shelter from the Storm* group can be led by either a professional counselor or a trained layperson. If you are a licensed counselor, communicate to your group that this is a support group, not a therapy group. If you are not a licensed counselor, establish a supervisory relationship with a licensed Christian counselor or pastoral counselor familiar with the issues of sexual abuse. Ask this person to discuss with you their clinical credentials and experience with survivors of sexual abuse. Find someone who is both clinically competent and theologically sound. Most Christian counselors will recognize the importance of this ministry and appreciate your need to have supervision and support while you are facilitating the group. You may be asked to pay a fee for this service. However, you may also be fortunate enough to find a Christian counselor in your area who would be willing to donate his or her time. You would need to arrange to meet with this person at least monthly while you are facilitating your group.

Step 6: Establish a Referral List

You will find information on the process of referral in the *LIFE Support Leader's Handbook* which contains a clear definition of referral, how to evaluate possible sources of assistance, and how to select a trustworthy counselor. Make a list of at least three competent professionals. Your small-group coordinator may already have developed a referral list. If not, follow the instructions in the handbook. Contact these individuals at least by phone and discuss with them your desire to provide their names to individuals in your group as possible resources.

Step 7: Decide on Child Care

Decide before promotion begins whether your church will offer child care for group members' children. The advantage of providing child care is that it will allow some to attend the group who might not be able to participate otherwise. The disadvantage is that support group sessions sometimes run late. If a group member needs special support or extra sharing time, it is important to have the freedom to let the needs of that member be priority. Group members also might be concerned about getting children home at a reasonable hour. Many find the best solution for support groups is to ask group members to secure child care on their own. Determine the needs of your people.

Step 8: Determine a format: Set a time and date for starting the group.

This may be your most difficult step. You will need to evaluate your own needs and limitations as well as those of your group and your church. Decide on a format for your group before you begin. See page 15 FG for more information about group format.

Set a date for the group to begin and set a starting time for the first session. After you meet you may want to adjust that time if another time is more convenient to your group members. Plan for at least 1-2 hours for each session. Depending on the format your group will follow, the group may meet for as few as 12 weeks or as long as a year.

Step 9: Decide on a location.

The group should meet in the same location each week. The meeting place needs to be private and free of distractions. It would be best if the room had an entrance away from the main entrance to the building so that group members could come and go without having to explain where they have been or where they are going. Often group members cry during sessions and need the security of knowing they can leave without having to reveal the source of their tears. Protect the confidentiality of the group by choosing the best time and location possible for the group.

The room should be clean, comfortable, and large enough to hold about eight chairs in a circle. To avoid a situation in which members feel trapped, when arranging chairs always leave a gap in the circle.

Never put a chair in front of the door. Make certain that outside observers cannot see into the room. Rest rooms should be accessible to the meeting room.

Choose a time when other activities at the church building are at a minimum. Children running and playing, choir rehearsal, or basketballs hitting a gym floor will cause group members to fear interruptions. They will not be able to focus on their issues and might be less likely to share. I do not recommend meeting in a home due to distractions, issues of liability, and confidentiality.

Step 9: Order materials
Order sufficient copies of the following materials well in advance of your first meeting.

Member's Book (item 7208-44), one copy for each group member
Facilitator's Guide (item 7209-44), one copy for yourself and one for your apprentice or co-facilitator

Materials may be purchased at a Baptist Book Store, Lifeway Christian Store, or ordered from the Customer Service Center; 127 Ninth Avenue, North; Nashville, TN 37234; 1-800-458-2772.

Step 10: Decide on promotional efforts
The need for confidentiality will affect how you choose to promote. You can find many ways to publicize the group.

Announce your group in your church publications. Make this announcement very positive. Emphasize hope and healing as well as confidentiality. Do not advertise the time and meeting room. Include the name and number of the contact person. Do not have a general request to call the church office.

Someone needs to serve as the telephone contact person for *Shelter*. The telephone contact person will receive calls from persons interested in the group. This person needs to be knowledgeable about the ministry. Do not have people simply call the church office. You may choose to receive the calls yourself or train your apprentice to do so. The duties for this person are outlined on page 17.

After your ministry is well established-a year or two-you may consider broadening the scope of your promotion. Some other ideas for promoting include-

- Submit information about your group to local newspapers. Many newspapers will print a brief news release (one to two paragraphs). If you can connect it to a recent news article or editorial you may be able to get more space.
- Contact local businesses and industries. We often overlook that local doctors, Employee Assistance Programs, hospitals, and government agencies look for resources for their people. *Shelter from the Storm* can be an outlet for ministry to the community.
- List your group in local social service directories. Find these by contacting city, county, or state social service offices or mental health agencies. Be sure you know the telephone number and person that can serve as a long-term contact.

Step 11: Set fees for materials
Gather your materials and determine how much you want to charge for each member. You may want to include enough money to cover expenses such as publicity, handouts, member books, or child care. If you offer scholarships, determine the criteria and percentage of the fee the church is willing to cover. Grant partial scholarships; individuals that pay even a small price for materials tend to demonstrate a stronger commitment to any type of group. Make sure any charge made for the group is directly related to materials. You create a liability issue if you charge for group attendance.

Step 12: Get Started
Review your materials and determine any last minute items you may have forgotten. Spend time in discussion and prayer with your support system as you prepare to meet with your group.

Group Format

Sexual abuse recovery groups are different than any other kind of group. The distinctives of a *Shelter from the Storm* group include-
- longer term
- closed groups
- necessity of a network of referral resources
- groups do not take breaks
- necessity of a co-facilitator
- emotional volatility of group members
- legal reporting requirements for certain situations must be observed.

Shelter from the Storm groups follow a closed group format. The group is closed to new members after the first or second session. A closed group usually meets for a pre-determined length of time. The group may then choose to re-form, opening the group to new members and beginning the cycle of materials again.

Two possible formats exist for conducting *Shelter*, the 12-week format and the extended format-from six months to one year. If you choose the 12-week format, be aware that the "Group Session" materials in this guide provide far more material than you ever can cover in a single session. Select only a few of the sharing questions or activities for a single session. If you choose the six-month or one-year format, use the same opening and closing for multiple sessions. The facilitator's guide contains material for multiple sessions.

Three 12-week cycles a year:
0 Advertise starting and ending date for each 12-week period.
0 Interview participants and describe the format for the group. Introduce them to the requirements of unit one.
0 Cover one unit each week.
0 Close the group to new members after the first meeting.
0 End the group on the date specified. Announce the date of the new group and invite members to consider taking another journey through *Shelter from the Storm.* You may want to invite them to function as support to new members or you may find that a member is ready to co-facilitate the next group with you.

.24-Week Cycle or 12-Month Cycles:
0 Advertise starting and ending date for the group.
0 Interview participants and describe format for the group. Introduce them to the requirements of unit 1.
0 Cover one unit every two weeks. Or if you have chosen the 12-month cycle cover one unit a month.
0 Close the group to new members after the second week. If you are on a 12-month cycle, you may close after the third week but do not allow new members to join the group after the group completes unit 1. Keep a waiting list. If that list reaches five, start a new group rather than add to the existing group.
0 End the group on the date specified. Announce the date of the formation of the new group and invite members to consider taking another journey through *Shelter from the Storm.* You may want to invite them to function as support to new members or you may find that a member is ready to co-facilitate the next group with you.

Group Size

A group should not exceed eight participants. The group should contain enough people to feel like a "group." It should be small enough that everyone has the opportunity to participate frequently. If your regis-

tration exceeds eight participants, consider establishing two groups or maintaining a waiting list for your next group. Encourage those who are waiting for a *Shelter* group to participate in another support group such as *Conquering Codependency* while they wait. You may also want to keep a list of other churches in your area that are facilitating *Shelter* groups.

Group Participants

Gender
Shelter will apply to both male and female survivors of sexual abuse . A *Shelter* group can be all male, all female, or a group of both males and females.

Advantages and disadvantages exist to both types of groups. Some group members would be less timid to talk about details of the abuse in an all-male or all-female group. Some survivors may have so much fear of the opposite sex that they will not be able *to* function in a mixed group.

Participation in a mixed group later in the recovery journey is helpful. Such groups have the advantage of providing an opportunity to hear support and encouragement from someone of the opposite sex. Mixed groups tend to encourage the individual to work through opposite-sex issues resulting from the abuse.

Age
Group members typically need to be at least 18 years of age. *Shelter* could be adapted for use with adolescents 13-18 in a group together. Do not combine adolescents and adults in the same group. The personal needs of each are too diverse.

Relationships

Spouses
Do not place spouses together in a group. Group members need freedom to share openly about the past and the present. A group member may need to talk about the effect of the abuse on present sexual behavior . The dynamics of the marital relationship would impact the process of the individual's recovery and that of the group.

Other Family Members
Do not place family members together in a group. This is especially true if the abuse was incest. Once again the dynamics of the family system would impact the process of the group. Family therapy is the appropriate context for family members to discuss incest.

Friendships

The member's book has information on the relationship issues that are often present in survivors. You will need to monitor and address the affect of close friendships on the group process.

Duties for the Telephone Contact Person

Enlist a telephone contact person to receive calls from people interested in the group. This person needs to have a clear understanding of the guidelines, format, and services your group can and will provide. For example you will need to determine if your group will involve victims of adult sexual abuse such as rape or molestation .

U you have enough interested people, divide victims of adult sexual abuse from those that were abused as children. While *Shelter from the Storm* addresses both situations, the issues are quite different. You may want to develop a script that will give you a guideline for the telephone contact person to follow.

A Sample Script: *"Shelter from the Storm* is a recovery program from the experience of being sexually abused as a child or adolescent. This is a Christ-centered group and will involve the use of Scripture and prayer. We cover the *Shelter from the Stann* process in a semester consisting of 12 weekly sessions. These semesters are repeated three times a year. You are asked to make a commitment to attend the entire 12 weeks unless special circumstances prevent you from attending. An example of a special circumstance would be a counselor recommending that you discontinue. At the end of each semester the group member will have the option to graduate, to take a break, or to return for the next session. Almost all members choose to continue for at least three semesters, but they can choose in 12-week increments. This means they will recycle through the issues addressed by *Shelter* three times and usually at three different levels of recover y. New group members can enter at the beginning of each new semester as room permits or as new groups are formed. Semesters are scheduled to begin on:

Semester one: (dates)
Semester two: (dates)
Semester three: (dates)

"All information shared in the group is confidential. No one comes 'to visit' a *Shelter* group. Members also cannot bring friends or relatives to the group. No one can enter the group after the first week of the 12-week semester."

Adapt this suggested script to fit the needs of your 24-week or 12-month group format.

When to Refer

Recognize your limitations as a facilitator and learn how to encourage a person to seek professional help. The symptoms listed below are serious and should not be minimized. Sometimes making a referral will cause the person to become angry or fearful. Helping members find the resources they need is your primary ministry if the following symptoms are present.

1. Suicidal Thoughts or Plans
- a lack of a desire to live
- urtcontrollable thoughts of hurting themselves in some manner
- feeling helpless or hopeless
- verbalizing a specific plan for hurting themselves
- individuals who have made previous suicide attempts

2. Homicidal Thoughts or Plans
- uncontrollable feelings of anger
- verbalizing a definite plan to injure or kill another person

3. Mood, Thought, or Character Disorders
- phobias
- obsessive-compulsive behaviors
- extreme anxiety
- hysteria
- extreme depression creating dysfunction in normal daily routine
- anorexia/bulimia
- arrested moral development
- delusions or hallucinations
- confusion of thought or speech
- inability to interpret reality
- bizarre or disorganized behaviors
- inability to respond emotionally

4. Substance Misuse and Abuse
- alcohol
- illegal drugs
- prescription drugs

5. Physical Symptoms
- extreme headaches
- any physical symptom that affects daily functioning

6. Any other problem you feel overwhelmed with due to the intensity of the problem or your own emotional, physical, spiritual capacity to be objective and helpful.

Special Considerations

Sexual abuse is an issue which includes special legal and ethical concerns. You need to be aware of your legal responsibilities for reporting certain situations to the authorities, and you need to advise prospective members in advance about the limits to confidentiality imposed by federal and state law.

Reporting Responsibilities
You are required by law to report certain issues to appropriate authorities. These include:
- a group member who threatens to do harm to self or others.
- a group member who is or has been involved in harm to a child or elderly person.

Because these laws vary from state to state, you have the responsibility to learn your specific reporting responsibilities. You may contact any of the following sources for information on the legal requirements in your state.
- Check with your supervisor. If you are a layperson, you should have a trained counselor as a supervisor. Your supervisor will be familiar with reporting responsibilities.
- Call your local psychiatric hospital.
- Call the government health and welfare department in your area.
- Call the local police department.
- Call a sexual abuse hotline.

Interview Prospective Group Members
Interview each prospective group member before the first group session. At that interview you can accomplish many important tasks.
- Explain the purpose and function of the group.
- Answer the person's questions.
- Advise the person of the limits to confidentiality.

On page 56 you will find a sample form called "Support Group Guidelines." Use this form or develop your own. You will avoid potential problems by making clear in advance the purposes and limitations of the group. Once new members have read the guidelines and signed the form showing their commitment to the group, permit them to pick up or purchase a copy of the member's book, *Shelter from the Storm*, and ask them to begin working on unit 1.

Ritualistic Sexual Abuse

Ritualistic sexual abuse (sometimes called satanic ritual abuse or SRA) is an issue that will affect some groups. Facilitators do not need to have the training to treat the disorders caused by this form of abuse, but they do need to be familiar with the issue. Victims of this form of abuse require referral to a professional counselor. Facilitators should never seek to treat these survivors.

Ritualistic sexual abuse represents the ultimate in human degradation . With an increased openness about sex in general, some people are beginning to identify the terrible ritualistic sexual abuse they have experienced. The abuse is a part of a satanic ritual. Sometimes the abusers are the child's own parents who are involved in a satanic cult. Other cases of abuse have occurred without the parent's knowledge.

A controversy surrounds the issue of ritualistic sexual abuse. Some assert that this issue has been sensationalized, and far too many people claim to be "victims." On the other hand, other authorities believe that threats make victims hide any evidence of the abuse. They believe that far more victims exist than those who have come forward so far.

Components of Ritualistic Sexual Abuse

Ritualistic sexual abuse is degrading, sadistic, and painful. It includes multiple sexual attacks from members of the group; insertion of painful instruments in body orifices; and/or forced sexual activity with animals, infants, or the dead .

Perpetrators use psychological abuse to gain total control over the victim. They use physical threats, coupled with physical tortures. Victims are forced to engage in repulsive, often illegal activities and then told this has sealed their fate as a cult member and that they can never be accepted in society again.

These perpetrators indoctrinate and brainwash their victims against their families-if their families do not belong to the cult-against church , and society in general. The purpose of these threats is to force the victims to believe that the only place they can exist is in the cult . Various mind-controlling techniques are utilized, such as food, water, and sleep-deprivation; long indoctrination sessions; use of drugs, threats, and torture; and programming for specific destructive activities.

Spiritual abuse involves forcing victims to participate in rituals and activities that induce the belief that they are totally separated from God and are totally controlled by Satan. They often are told that they have spirit demons that will control them and punish them if they fail to obey. The younger a person is when ritual abuse begins, the greater the emotional damage and the likelihood of being incorporated into the cult's beliefs and actions.

Uncertain, Prognosis

Without professional help, the outcome for victims of ritual sexual abuse is often grim. Many become so brainwashed that they remain in the cult as abusers themselves. Those who get away from the perpetrators and try to live a normal life are plagued with a host of physical, emotional, spiritual, and behavioral problems. These people are often treated for psychosomatic illnesses, hysteria, depression, phobias, panic attacks, obsessions, schizophrenia, and other personality disorders. If the underlying trauma from the abuse is not treated, they will never experience adequate healing. Unfortunately, the underlying trauma may not even be remembered . It may seem incredible that such horrible abuse could be forgotten. Ironically, the very mental mechanism that helps people survive this kind of trauma also can block conscious recall years later. This phenomenon is called *dissociation*.

Dissociation

If a person is overwhelmed with severe abuse, torture, or terror, particularly during childhood, the protective mechanisms of dissociation may come into play. These people assume an altered state of consciousness in which they "dissociate" or separate themselves from the agonizing event-as though they are somewhere else and the abuse is happening to a different person.

The ability to dissociate is not entirely negative . It actually protects the victim from being totally overwhelmed . Dissociation takes many forms including depersonalization, derealization, and multiple personality disorder.

Depersonalization

Depersonalization is a frightening experience. The person is completely aware of what is taking place. These individuals feel as if they are suddenly outside their bodies, as if they are observing some other person interacting with the environment. They may describe the feeling as if they were in a dream or were a robot. They may have no feeling in various parts of the body and be unable to control their speech and behavior.

Derealization

Derealization is a phenomenon in which the environment suddenly seems altered or dreamlike, but the person maintains his or her own sense of personal reality, unless depersonalization occurs, which is not uncommon. Size and shape of things may change; people may seem to be robots or dead, or phantoms of some sort.

Multiple Personality Disorder

In multiple personality disorder (MPD), a person has many separate identities-or personality fragments-known or unknown to each other. The basic goal in treating multiple personality disorder is to integrate the alter personalities (referred to as *alters*). Each alter has special feelings, roles, and reactions, and each has developed a response to severe trauma.

The counselor's goal is to help the person to understand that even the most negative alters have positive aspects and certainly, positive potential; thus the goal is not to get rid of a basic part, but to have a healthy integration so the positive traits of the different alters can add up to an improved whole. Some MPD clients already know about some of the alters and can switch from one to the other on request, and sometimes the switch simply occurs spontaneously.

MPD represents a unique opportunity to bring healing at a significantly deep level. This healing process requires a counselor specifically trained and experienced in MPD counseling. A person with MPD can be greatly harmed if powerful memory fragments and alters become a chaotic, overpowering experience. If you encounter MPD, make an appropriate referral to a qualified counselor.

Support from a Christian Group

Survivors of ritualistic sexual abuse need professional assistance. In addition, they need a new, powerful, loving, supportive group to promote further healing and correction from having been involved in a horribly destructive group. These survivors need a group of nurturing Christians who understand this condition and who do not short-circuit the healing process with cliches and instant cures. Unenlightened Christian groups have often caused damage by casting out nonexistent demons and giving advice as if some magical cure could come with the right attitude or the right phrases spoken as prayer.

All of us, particularly recovering abuse victims, are engaged in spiritual warfare, and the ultimate victory comes through the grace and power of Jesus Christ. What people with dissociative disorders need is a slow and thorough explanation of all the facets of the abuse and their reactions to it, engagement of the multiple personalities with the ultimate goal of gaining their cooperation, and finally integrating them into the total person. Professional care-along with prayer and the acceptance of God's grace, love, and forgiveness-can bring hope and wholeness.

Dealing with Control and Anger

First-time facilitators may be emotionally unprepared for two facets of sexual abuse recovery-the controlling behaviors and the overwhelming anger of their group members.

Sexual abuse is among the most severe forms of boundary violation. In the abuse experience, the perpetrator took away the survivor's sense of self-control. The survivor then seeks to regain the loss of safety by controlling the environment, self, and others.

Anger is a normal and healthy response to the experience of sexual abuse. Unfortunately, the victim usually has not been allowed to express that anger appropriately and direct it toward the person who was responsible, so the anger can become generalized or free floating, and the survivor may turn the anger on anyone, including-if not especially-the person who is seeking to help.

As a facilitator, you need to be aware of the dual problems of control and anger. A group member may blast you with her anger, or you may feel confused by her powerful efforts to control you or the group. At the very least you need to avoid taking the anger and control personally. As you grow in the skills of group leadership, you can become better able to manage group members who are controlling.

Managing angry and manipulative members is a challenge. Recognize the source of the anger and that it is a natural, God-given response. If they have not learned to direct the anger toward its source, you can help them learn to focus the anger and to deal with it in more productive ways.

Recognize that attempts to control result from fear; they are a learned response. Survivors have maintained the illusion of safety by controlling some area of their lives. The group process poses a major threat: the fear of knowing and being known can be terrifying. Some group members will do almost anything to avoid facing the fear.

One group member may control the group by arriving late to every meeting. Another may control by talking all of the time. At times a member may hide behind a defensive wall of anger or may criticize you and your leadership.

Coping with Anger and Control

Survivors of sexual abuse have damaged boundaries and need to see good boundaries modeled and practiced. One of your tasks as facilitator is to set and maintain good boundaries. Start the group on time and end on time, not out of the need for a rigid schedule, but because you are learning to live with healthy limits.

Explain to the group that one of the tasks of the group is to learn to respect other people's boundaries . Explain, in advance, that you may have to enforce some boundaries such as limiting one member's time so that all members will have an opportunity to share. Explain that you are willing to risk angry reactions if necessary. ·

As in all areas of group leadership, be confessional. Explain that you have to work to practice good boundaries in your own life. Group members will respond more favorably when they see you as a fellow struggler.

You will encounter both anger and controlling behavior as you facilitate groups. Keep in mind the following steps for dealing with controlling and angry behavior:

1. Anticipate manipulative behavior. It is normal. It is natural, and it is common. You need to know that it is coming and that it comes in many forms.
2. Recognize the behaviors when they appear.
3. Talk to your supervisor about techniques to deal with the behaviors.
4. Respond appropriately to these challenges in the group. Do not overreact, blow up, or withdraw. Be calm and direct. Affirm the person who is being manipulative but confront the behavior.
5. Use these instances in the group as process issues so that everyone in the group can learn.

Overview of Group Sessions

The following group session plans have been prepared to assist you in your preparation for each week's session. An overview of the format for the group session plans appears below. How you choose to use these plans will depend on the time schedule and format you have chosen for your group.

Unit Goal. Whether your group covers each unit in one week, two weeks, or one month, the goal for that unit will remain the same. Your use of this material will need to be suited to the needs of your group as God has led you to see those needs and respond to them. You will have goals for each session but be prepared for the Holy Spirit to intervene and minister in a way that you did not expect. God knows the needs of your group members better than you do. Your group members will hear more than you or other group members are saying as the Lord moves in the midst of your group. You cannot know enough to facilitate your group alone, but with the presence of the Holy Spirit, you can!

What to Expect: In this section you will find information to prepare you for the attitudes and behaviors typical of a particular issue or developmental stage of the group. Predicting individual and group responses are not always possible, but some topics generally raise certain responses.

Skill Development: The information in this section is based upon the assumption that you have facilitated a support group, participated in LIFE® Support Group Series leadership training, or at least read and studied the *Life Support Leader's Handbook*. If not, please consider this a request to do so. I will be referring to the *Handbook* as a major resource. There will be suggestions in each unit for you to review and practice your basic skills as a facilitator. I also encourage you to obtain a copy of *Conquering Codependency: A Christ Centered 12-Step Process* member's book and facilitator's guide as a resource for family of origin issues. These may be ordered by calling 1-800-458-2772. Ask for product numbers 7200-33 and 7201-33.

Before the Session: Each unit will have a checklist to help you determine your readiness to facilitate that unit. If you are spending more than one week on each session you will want to review this list prior to each meeting time. Place a check mark beside each item as you complete it. After a few sessions you will find that many of the items will become routine since they are repeated each session; however, there will be changes so don't forget to review the list for each unit.

During the Session: Your group members need to have a general idea of what to expect each time they come to a meeting. A structured environment will help the group members feel safe and secure. Give your group members a few minutes to check in and debrief from the previous session, but do not allow the group to deviate from the purpose for being there. Some sexual abuse survivors will find any excuse to keep from talking about the abuse. Others will talk too readily, giving too much information too quickly or sensationalizing their stories to get attention. Survivors of sexual abuse n ed to identify and own their feelings without explanation or apology. They will unconsciously attempt to keep off the subject at hand because it is so painful. Each group session will close with a look at the unit Scriptures and with prayer.

Each unit of this facilitator 's guide contains more material than you can cover in a single week or even in several weeks. I suggest that the group work through the book in 12 sessions, with the understanding that members will benefit most from participating in three groups, each meeting for 12 weeks. Thus members will cycle through the material three times, first to understand and then deeply apply the material to their recovery. This plan calls for a minimum of 36 weeks in the process.

If you use the suggested plan, you will select only a few of the activities and sharing topics for each unit. Others may conclude that they desire to spend more than one group session on each unit. Either method will work. Consider your situation and prayerfully decide how you will conduct the group.

Af ter th e Session: The checklist on the inside back cover will help you to evaluate the needs of the group and your effectiveness as a group facilitator. After each session take some time to work through this checklist and pray about the needs of your group and your role as facilitator. If you are co-facilitating the group, take time together to talk about this list and set goals for the next session.

A Foundation for Recovery

Session Goal: Group members will-
- describe the process of recovery;
- discover areas where they are already experiencing recovery;
- identify how to set goals for recovery in other areas of their lives;
- develop a support system before continuing their participation in the support group.

What to Expect:

In the early stages of group development, the members and the group as a whole will experience tension around the issues of goals, belonging, safety and security, authority, and identity.
- *Goals-What do I want from this group? What am I supposed to do here? Are the goals of the group the same as my goals? Will my personal concerns be heard?*
- *Belonging-How do I fit in this group? What will it cost me to belong? What group pressures do I feel? How much can I accept from others? How much am I willing to give to others?*
- *Safety and Security-Is it safe to share in this group? What will the group do if I let them know me? How open can I be with the group? How much risk am I willing to take? How much trust can I honestly express to others?*
- *Authority-Who is in charge in this group? How will that person react toward me and my issues? How am I going to react toward them?*
- *Identity-Who am I in this group? What is my role? Who are the other people? What kind of behavior is acceptable in this group?*

Communicate that you recognize these issues. You may feel the fear as the group members enter the room. Some group members may linger in the hall before coming into the room. Some may leave rather than risk coming into the group. Communicate that you understand that the group has gathered to talk about a very difficult subject. Also communicate that you believe that to talk about their sexual abuse in the group is safe and that the group is going to start now. If you hesitate you will increase their anxiety. Expect them to be anxious and afraid. Remember that the group must learn to share and accept feelings.

Skill Development

Teach your group members how to give appropriate feedback. One of your most important tasks is to train the group members in this skill.

Explain that feedback is a loving and supportive form of communication. Because we cannot see ourselves objectively, we need honest friends who can help us to perceive our thoughts and behaviors in an unbiased way.

State the foundational rule for feedback in the group: *Members will request permission before giving feedback. Any person has the right to grant or refuse permission for feedback-we do not violate each other's boundaries by giving feedback without permission.*

Explain that feedback can reflect feelings or restate information to check for accuracy. Survivors develop mechanisms to cope with the trauma of sexual abuse. They learn to numb their feelings. They lose the ability to connect their feelings with the source event or thought. The feedback process helps us listen for feelings and support survivors in the process of naming their feelings. Examples of appropriate feedback responses include-
- "Help me understand how that feels to you."
- "Can you identify how that feels?"
- "And how do you feel when that happens?"

Feedback is stated in a positive manner. Empathizing will communicate care. Survivors believe others cannot understand what happened to them or how they feel about it. You can model for the group how to respond in an empathetic way. Be careful that you don't interpret what group members share. The following statements reflect what not to say.
- "If that had happened to me, I would have felt..."
- "That feeling is appropriate to the situation you were in."
- "It sounds to me as if you were feeling...."

Feedback needs to be encouraging. Survivors need for you to encourage them without discounting their pain by trying to cheer them up. The best encouragement is support.

Say things like:
- "This is a difficult time for you, but you can get through it. Can you identify your strength and hope for this situation?"
- "How can we support you?"
- "What has helped you through times like this in the past?"

Before the Session

O Read and complete the learning activities for unit 1 in *Shelter from the Storm* member's book.

O If you are providing child care, confirm arrangements. Because the first session may run a little longer than other sessions, make sure that workers are prepared to stay as late as necessary.

O Check the church calendar to make sure that you have the room requested and for the length of time requested. You do not want people arriving for another meeting as you are completing your group time.

O Contact group members to make sure they know when and where you are meeting. This will also give you an opportunity to respond to last-minute questions and anxious reservations.

O Make sure the room is clean and chairs are arranged in a circle with just enough to accommodate your group. Remember to leave a gap in the circle of chairs and do not place a chair in fran t of the door. A void creating a feeling of being trapped.

O Provide several boxes of tissues.

O Have tear sheets and markers available for use during the session.

O Photocopy the Scripture/Affirmation cards (page 58) on card stock. When your group is ready to move to the next unit, provide one Scripture/Affirmation card for each group member for the upcoming unit. Provide a card for wl it 1 and unit 2 at this first group meeting.

O Provide a copy of the Supporter's Packet for each member of the group. This material can be found on pages 59-61 FG.

During the Session

The structure for this session is the same for all groups regardless of choice of format. The first group session needs to be structured to flow without great lapses of silence. Long periods of silence can be beneficial and healthy at later stages of group life, but this first session needs to move forward. Silence will intensify the anxiety already present in the group.

Arrival-Greet the group members as they arrive for the session. Give each member a support group affirmations card.

Start-Set an example for promptness by beginning on time.
- Read the Welcome Statement (page 57 FG). Reading the Welcome Statement each week will help the group stay focused on its purpose. In this session it will set the stage for the rest of your time together. You will demonstrate from the beginning that this group is going to talk about sexual abuse.
- Introduce yourself. Tell the group how you became the facilitator of this group. If you are a survivor, you may want to share a portion of your recovery journey at this time. Use the analogy of a storm and how you found shelter from the storm of sexual abuse. If you are not a survivor of sexual abuse, relate the analogy to shelter from other storms in your life.
- Ask the group members to introduce themselves.
- Ask the group members what it means to them to have this group called "Shelter from the Storm."
- Ask: *What do you hope to receive from this support group?* Ask someone to record the responses on the flip chart. Remove this sheet and place it on the wall with masking tape.
- Ask: *What do you hope to accomplish in this support group?* Record these responses on another flip chart sheet. Remove this sheet and place it on the wall with masking tape. Compare this list to the "Indications of Recovery" in your Supporter's Packet.
- Ask: *What are you expecting to happen when you start talking about the sexual abuse?* Record these responses on a tear sheet. It is important that these expectations become visible.

Talk about the process of recovery using material from unit 1. Focus on the need for support as necessary to break out of silence and isolation. You may want to use this analogy: When small children fall and hurt themselves, they usually run to someone and cry. That person will in some way attend to the hurt, probably by cleaning, medicating, and bandaging the wound. Most of us who have been sexually abused have never had our wound attended. We need to let go and allow others to help as we tend the wound. As survivors, we need to develop a support system within the group and with significant other people.

Explain that, for your sake and for theirs, you must not be any group member's sole support! The group member s need to know that you will not support any tendency to isolate. That is why naming a family member or significant other person who you can call in case of emergency is a requirement for joining the group. Another requirement for joining the group is some type of relationship with a counselor. Do not allow someone to place you in the position of caretaker!

Give each group member a copy of the Supporter's Packet and talk to them about the role of a support person. Prepare them for both positive and negative reactions. Someone may be unwilling to be a support person for them. They need to be able to accept this without taking it personally. Discuss some of the reasons a prospective support person might say no. (Schedule, other personal demands, feelings of inadequacy, personal recovery issues, etc.)

- Go over the list of Do's and Don'ts for a support person.
- Ask: *Do you have a friend or family member that you could trust enough to say: "I am a survivor of sexual abuse. I am going to join a* Shelter *support group. Pray for me while I take this important step in my life."*

Allow the group members to talk about how this feels for them. This is a difficult step. Be gentle, but do not take no for an answer. To have an enlisted and identified support person is an absolute condition for group membership. If they cannot tell at least one member of their family, they probably are not ready for this type of group. You need for them to have more support than you can provide. The other person may be their counselor or therapist, but they need to have a support person outside the group. As a facilitator, you need to have a list of the supporter's names in case of an emergency. Later you will want to ask, "Have you talked to _____ lately?" Especially when the group member starts to be too dependent on you. This is an important issue for you and your group.

- Ask the group members to name their support person(s) or prospective support person(s).
- Ask members how they expect this person to react when they ask them to be their support person.

Use the memory verse to communicate that two sources of support exist. The ultimate and complete source is God. Other people who understand and care are the second source. Ask someone to read the memory verse.

> *I said, "Oh, that I had the wings of a dove! I would fly away and be at rest-I would flee far away and stay in the desert; I would hurry to my place of shelter, far from the tempest and storm" (Psalm 55:6-8, NASB).*

Share what this passage of Scripture means to you. Invite others to share.

- *What does it mean to have a "shelter from the storm"?* Refer the group to the list on tear sheet 1.

- Read the affirmation for the unit. Ask your group members to say it with you.
- Read this passage of Scripture and close with prayer.

> *I will go before you and make the rough places smooth; I will shatter the doors of bronze, and cut through their iron bars. And I will give you the treasures of darkness, and hidden wealth of secret places, in order that you may know that it is I, the Lord, the God of Israel, who calls you by your name.*
>
> -Isaiah 45: 2-3, NASB

Say: *God is the one who will make the rough places smooth. Recovery involves opening up some areas that are dark and frightening. It involves revealing information that has been kept secret. God can help you find treasures in the darkness and wealth in those secret places. You need to know that you exist and have meaning and value. God calls YOU by NAME!*

Pray for your group and mention each person by name. Begin to teach your group the "Serenity Prayer." Refer to page 157 in the member's book. Close your prayer time with the Serenity Prayer.

After the Session

O Write down each group member's name. Before the next group session, pray for each member specifically. Pray for members with special needs.

O Call each group member. Encourage him or her in the preparation for the next session. Ask if they have prayed about whom to ask to be their support person and if they are preparing to contact them. Provide any encouragement needed. Reinforce the importance of obtaining support for themselves. Assure members that you will pray for them to follow through on this assignment.

O Make a copy of the leader worksheet, "Evaluating Each Session"(inside back cover). Use this to assess the first session. If you have an apprentice, fill in and discuss this worksheet with him or her.

O Discuss with your supervisor or your apprentice the dynamics of the group process.

O Read "Before the Session" for Group Session 2, and carefully complete all the activities in unit 2 of the member's book, if you are ready to move to that session. If you are using a multiple sessions per unit format, review the materials for Group Session 1 to prepare for your next group.

Discovering Hope

Session Goal: Group members will-
- define sexual abuse and identify experiences in their life that were abusive;
- begin to understand their feelings and behaviors in a different way;
- begin to identify the mechanisms that allowed them to survive the abuse as symptoms of sexual abuse.

What to Expect

Your group still will be dealing with the issues related to stage one of group development. Do not expect them to have resolved those issues. As a facilitator you will benefit from a review (see page 11 FG).

- Members will be concerned about what they want and need from the group. They will wonder if their wants and needs will be addressed. You cannot guarantee that their needs will be met, but as a group facilitator you can see that they are addressed. Ask yourself, "Are we doing what we are here as a group to do-to support one another in recovering from sexual abuse?"
- Your group may begin to form subgroups. Be careful that you give everyone a chance to respond. Support the value of everyone in the group.
- Some members will feel like they said too much last time. They will be asking such questions as, *Am I really safe? Now what do they think about me?* Others will be testing to see if they can feel comfortable enough to begin to share.
- All eyes will be on you to see how you react-especially how you deal with talking about sexual abuse. Members will wonder if you can deal with hearing what happened to them. If you give the appearance that you don't want to talk about sexual abuse, they will not talk about it. They want you to be in charge. Members know they do not know how to talk about abuse. They are expecting you to lead the way. Your sharing gives members permission to share; your example is crucial. Your role will not be as critical later as other members participate more.

Your group members will be struggling with their own identities in the group: *Can I cry here? Can I scream? Can I be me, or do I pretend?*

Skill Development

Establish clear boundaries with your group members.
- Group members need you to define your boundaries. How can you have the boundaries you need so that you do not get overwhelmed by the needs of the group?
- You want to be supportive and encouraging, but you will do group members no favor by caretaking and fixing. The key is to communicate clearly what you are willing to do. State your boundaries.
- In the first session you need to communicate to your group exactly how available you are willing to be.

When a group member steps across the boundary you set, you need to immediately remind them and reinforce the boundary. For example, a group member who starts calling you every day or every other day does not have enough support and is taking advantage of your availability. Survivors of sexual abuse have more needs than you alone can provide.

Do not establish a pattern of responding in the middle of the night or of dropping everything you are doing to run to the need of a group member. This will set both of you up for failure. Members must learn to depend on themselves and on God, not you! This is why the "Plan to Manage Crisis" (inside back cover FG) includes a list of supporters. Train members to call you *after* they have talked to others in their support system.

Encourage members to verbalize their solutions. Sometimes it feels as if it would be easier to just tell members what to do. Do not do it! You will keep them from discovering their own self-sufficiency. It would be easier to make a cake yourself than to teach children to make their own. But if you make it yourself the children gain nothing and will eventually resent you for not letting them do it themselves. Group members will eventually resent you for not allowing them to struggle for their own recovery. You can't do it for them, regardless of how much you care.

Focus on options survivors have for themselves. Find out what they have done for themselves. Guide them to discover what they can do for themselves.

Responding to a group member in crisis
- Listen and identify why the member called.
- Listen for feelings. Is the member communicating a sense of direction or of desperation, hopelessness, and helplessness?

One symptom of sexual abuse is a learned helplessness . Victims genuinel y get trapped in their own method of thinking about the world. When abuse colors the way survivors experience the world, they are not aware that they do not have to be a victim any longer. Part of supporting survivors of sexual abuse is encouraging them as they take charge of their own lives. If you carry them, they will never learn that they can carry themselves.

When you are called by a member who appears to be in crisis, ask these questions:
- "Are you safe? What can you do to be safe?"
- "Have you told anyone in your family that you are having this problem?"
- "What do you think will be helpful? What has been helpful in the past?"
- "Have you talked to your counselor about it?" If the answer is no, ask, "Why not?"

If the group member is suicidal or homicidal, take immediate action. Inform his or her emergency-contact person.

Block inappropriate feedback
Your task is to train members in the skill of honest and loving communication. One of your most difficult but most important jobs will be to stop group members from giving inappropriate feedback. Inappropriate feedback includes-
- Feedback that has not been requested or granted
- Statements that imply or convey judgment
- Statements that are disrespectful of a person's feelings, opinions, or self-esteem

Before the Session

O Read and complete the learning activities for unit 2 in the member's book.
O Make sure the room is clean and the chairs are arranged in a circle with enough to accommodate your group. Remember to leave an exit gap in the circle to avoid the feeling of being trapped.
O Have a flip chart and markers available for use during the session.
O Prepare Scripture/Affirmation cards for unit 3.
O Contact group members to encourage them and address any fears, reservations, and expectations.
O Provide several boxes of tissues for the room.

During the Session

Arrival-Greet everyone by name. Start on time.

Checking In-
- Ask someone to read the Welcome Statement.
- Ask members if they would like to share anything about last week's group. Allow members to share thoughts that will support someone else. Encourage both concerns and celebrations.
- Ask members to give you the copies of their "Plan for Managing Crisis" if they have not already done so. Remind them that the "Plan for Managing Crisis" is not optional. They must complete it to continue in the group.

Encourage members to talk about their experience with the crisis plan. Was it more difficult or easier than they expected? How did their supporters respond when asked and given a Supporter's Packet? Be prepared for both positive and negative responses . Remind members that they cannot control others. People respond the way they do for many reasons. Most of the time people's responses reflect their situations and needs rather than how they feel about the survivor and the survivor's issues. Say: *One of the reasons people respond the way they do* is *that many people do not have an accurate definition of sexual abuse.*

Share Time-Ask someone to volunteer to read the definition of sexual abuse (page 26).
- Allow the group to share their feelings about the definition. Ask if there are any questions about the definition .
- Read or ask someone to read the portion of Cindy's story recorded in unit 1 (page 25).
- Share how you felt while listening to Cindy's story. Guide the group to share their feelings. Ask if a group member would like to respond to how they felt. Listen for feelings of sadness, anger, numbness, or fear.
- Ask, *Would someone like to share how what happened to them was similar to or different from what happened to Cindy?*
- Ask the group members to turn to page 28 and identify the factor that prevented them from being able to choose to say no to their abuser.

    O Age
    O Level of understanding
    0 Dependency /relationship to offender
    O Fear of consequences
    O Physical strength or intimidation
    O Other _____

- Ask them to describe what their relationship was to the offender. If they did not know the person who abused them, what were the circumstances surrounding the abuse?

Lead a discussion on the types of sexual abuse (page 29). You might write the types on a chalkboard or a tear sheet. Ask members to name examples under each category. Ask for any comments they might have. Were they surprised by anything on the list?
- Ask your group to respond to this statement:. *Sexual abuse often begins with non-contact types of abuse that invade the emotional and psychological boundaries of the victim before the abuser makes any attempt to cross physical boundaries.*
- Ask, *What are some examples?* The answers should include suggestive comments, dirty jokes, unwant- ed exposure to pornography, etc. When confronted, the offender may treat the victim as though they had misunderstood the intent . The offender may claim that the victim is overreacting or being a prude. The victim is shamed for not wanting or lik- ing the behavior.

Invite members to share an experience like those just described.

Ask the group to help you create a list of the symptoms of sexual abuse. Ask for a volunteer to write the responses on the tear sheet. Allow them to look at the book if necessary . If you are a survivor, share with the group any of these symptoms that have been a part of your experience. Then ask the group to talk about their experiences. Describe any areas of growth. Which ones continue to be a problem?

Take time to pray as a group. Ask God to help you accept that these symptoms are results of the abuse. Ask God to begin to resolve the trauma from the abuse. Thank God right now for what is going to happen as each of you seek to find healing.

Ask someone to read Cindy's responses from page 39. Ask for the group members' reactions to the story.

As a group read the "The Overcomer's Hopes" (page 36).
- Watch for members' reactions to the reading. Allow members to respond spontaneously. If you are using a multiple session format, you may have time to add to this list on a tear sheet.

Review the Scripture by asking group members to share what Psalm 103:4-5 meant to them this week.

Close with a prayer. Give God permission to begin to renew group members so that they can soar like eagles. End with a group reading of the "Serenity Prayer."

After the Session

O Pray for each member specifically. Pray for group members with special needs.

O Call each group member. Encourage him or her in the study of the appropriate materials for the next session. Ask if they have prayed about their support person(s) and if they are preparing to contact them. Provide any encouragement needed. Reinforce the importance of obtaining support for themselves . Assure members that you will pray for them to follow through on this assignment.

O If you have allowed .a group member to begin unit 2 without obtaining additional support, make sure that you communicate that they must complete their support-system assignment if they are to continue with the group. They must have enlisted someone who will be a resource for them outside of the group.

O Use your copy of "Evaluating Each Session" (inside back cover) for this session. If you have an apprentice, fill in and discuss this worksheet with him or her.

O Discuss with your supervisor or your apprentice the dynamics of the group process.

O Read "Before the Session" for Group Session 3 and carefully complete all the activities in the member's book for unit 3, if you are ready to move to that session. If you are using a multiple sessions per unit format, review the materials for Group Session 2 to prepare for your next group.

Tell Yourself the Truth

Session Goal: Group members will begin to-
- understand that low self-esteem, illegitimate guilt, and undeserved responsibility for the abuse can be overcome;
- confront the false beliefs that are a result of the abuse experience.

What to Expect

Low self-esteem is a widespread problem among survivors of sexual abuse and generally is a fairly safe topic to talk about. You can anticipate that some of your quieter group members may be feeling like they belong. They may be willing to use this opportunity to risk being vulnerable to the group. However, the false beliefs addressed in this unit have served as defense mechanisms for some of your group members for many years. You may find some intense reactions to verbalizing and confronting these beliefs.

Many group members may have begun to realize that they have been in denial about the deep effects that the sexual abuse has had on their lives. They may be feeling more anxiety. Some may have revealed a secret that they have carried for years. They feel uncomfortable about being exposed. Explain that most survivors feel worse when they first begin to talk about the abuse. Explain that they can expect to feel better as they continue to face the feelings. The negative feelings begin to lose their power when they are exposed to the support and encouragement of those who care.

Group members also may be feeling intense grief. The sadness that comes with realizing the losses related to sexual abuse can be very painful. Help your group members recognize that grief is a process and it will reach a point of completion even though at times it feels like it will go on forever. Now is the time to provide understanding and hope.

Skill Development

Learn to confront without confronting! Confrontations are necessary with survivors of sexual abuse but should be made with special care and concern. You can confront without being aggressive. Simply reflect what you see and hear. In other words be a mirror. Learn to describe-without interpretation-just what you see group members doing or hear them saying.

For example, you have a group member who says that everything is great, but you see a deeply furrowed brow, or you see a tissue being twisted and torn. Rather than saying that you don't believe the member or that the member looks anxious to you, be a mirror. A mirror just describes; it does not interpret. "I hear you saying that you are doing great. I am glad to hear that; however, I noticed that while you were telling me you were great, you were twisting and tearing the tissue in your hand." Then wait. If the group member doesn't respond, go on. Don't probe. Don't interpret the experience. That is not your job as a support group facilitator. You have provided support and an opportunity for the member to talk. The group member may have realized with your perceptual feedback that he or she is not "great." The individual does not need to be forced to talk, but rather needs to be given the freedom to choose whether to respond to the feedback. You have also demonstrated that you will be honest about what you see without trapping or cornering members.

Other examples include:
- Talking about a very traumatic incident with no feeling evidenced. "I noticed that you were very still as you told us about that incident. Your facial expression did not change. Your voice tone was very soft. You did not cry."
- Smiling when talking about a hurt or pain. "I noticed that you smiled right before and right after you shared that with us."
- Speaking very softly. "I could barely hear you when you started talking about what your uncle said to you."
- Speaking very rapidly. "When you started talking about what it felt like to lie in bed and wait to see if she was coming, you began to speak very fast."

Learn the skill of giving perceptual feedback without interpretation. When you interpret a group member's behavior, you risk engaging defenses. If you will only give perceptual feedback, they have to interpret their own experience and in turn become more connected to themselves and to validating themselves.

Don't be afraid of times of silence. Group members may need time for reflection, to process deep emotions, to gather their thoughts, or to identify feelings.

Before the Session

O Read and complete the learning activities for unit 3 in the member's book.
O Have a flip chart and markers available for use during the session.
O Prepare Scripture/Affirmation cards for unit 4.
O Check room arrangement.
O Provide several boxes of tissues.

During the Session

Arrival-
• Greet everyone by name.
• Start on time.

Checking In-
• Ask someone to read the Welcome Statement.
• Ask if anyone has anything they would like to share about last week's group.

Share Time-
During this time you want members to identify the false beliefs that are keeping them trapped in shame, guilt, and undeserved responsibility for the abuse. When a person is sexually abused the experience tears apart the entire fabric of that person's life. You want members to see how these beliefs represent their effort to reweave the fabric.

Present the following material to the group-
Read the first two paragraphs from page 43 of the member's book.
• Say: *The experience of the sexual abuse victim is contrary to the way the world is supposed to be. We all carry some basic beliefs about how relationships are supposed to work. For example, fathers do not act sexually with their daughters, youth directors do not have intercourse with girls in their youth groups, Girl Scout counselors do not bring pornography to Brownie meetings, and my husband's best friend would not rape me. These behaviors are contrary to the reality of the world as we would like it to be. Therefore, victims distort their belief systems to blame themselves rather than deal with the pain of the loss of safety, security, and sometimes the relationship with an important person.*
• As a result, sexual abuse victims struggle with four major false beliefs about the abuse. List these false beliefs on four separate tear sheets.

1) It's my fault.
2) I must be a bad person for him/her to do this to me.
3) I wanted him or her to do this to me.
4) It didn't happen! I must have made it up.

• Say: *In this lesson and the next, we will explore examples and causes of these false beliefs.*
• Give each group member a marker, and ask them to write under the false belief any reasons or causes for that belief. They are to use their own knowledge as well as information from the text. They are free to talk to each other or to ask questions as they do this.
• After everyone has finished, guide the group in an open discussion about their answers.
• Ask members to share the false belief(s) with which they struggle.
• Start with false belief 1. Ask if anyone would share how they completed the sentence "It is my fault because   ." Ask for the contrasting truth statement. If the group member cannot make a truth statement, ask the group to help. This is very supportive.
• Ask for an example of false belief 2. Ask again for
the contrasting truth statement.

Write this sentence on a tear sheet. "Victims often try to hold onto the positive aspects of the relationship with the abuser by viewing themselves as dirty and undeserving of respect." Ask members to discuss what this sentence means to them.

Review the three major emotional consequences to sexual abuse. In lesson three we learned these are low self-esteem, guilt/self-blame, and shame. Discuss their relationship to the false beliefs.

Reproduce the "Cycle of False Beliefs" (page 62 FG) on a tear sheet or a marker board so that the group can see it, or copy and distribute the handout. Explain to the group that a destructive circular pattern emerges between the false beliefs and the resulting emotions. The shameful feelings cause the victim to believe that the shameful beliefs are valid. As this circle repeats itself, it becomes stronger and covers up the real person of value and worth whom God created. Victims ultimately lose touch with themselves in order to survive the pain and loss of the abuse.

Watch the reaction of the group to this experience. You may want to ask for feelings if the group is not responding with feeling words. Remember a feeling statement is, "I feel angry," or "I feel sad." A statement like, "I feel like a volcano" is a description, not a feeling statement. A feeling statement can be replaced with "I am_____."

If you have time, talk about the difference between shame and legitimate guilt.

- Guilt allows for making amends. If I break a glass, I am guilty of breaking the glass. I can correct the wrong by replacing the glass as soon as possible without shaming myself. Guilt allows for making amends.
- Shame involves judging myself negatively with no option to correct the judgment. "I am so stupid and clumsy. I can't believe I can't even walk across a room without dropping something!" The false beliefs result in shame and illegitimate or inappropriate guilt.

Review the focal passage for the unit. Ask group members what this Scripture means to them in light of the first two false beliefs.

Do not conform any longer to the pattern of this world, but be transformed by the renewing of your mind. Then you will be able to test and approve what God's will is-his good, pleasing, and perfect will.
-Romans 12:2

Read the memory verse. Ask the group to quote it with you. This is an important verse, and you will use it many times as your group members learn to speak the truth to themselves and others.

You will know the truth, and the truth will set you free.
-John 8:32

Ask: *What is the truth that will set you free?* Wait for a response. Allow discussion. Encourage feelings.

- In John 8:31-32 Jesus spoke of His teachings. He said that if we hold to His teaching, we would really be His disciples.
- We need to accept, believe, and base our lives on the truth rather than our distorted perceptions.
- His truth includes assigning appropriate responsibility by rejecting these false beliefs about sexual abuse.
- In this instance, the truth that will set us free is the truth about the sexual abuse.

You might also ask: *What is freedom?* Listen for realistic answers. Redirect unrealistic ones.

Close with a prayer circle. Ask someone to read the prayer in lesson 5 (page 55). End with the "Serenity Prayer."

After the Session

O Pray for each member specifically. Pray for group members with special needs.

O Call each group member. Encourage him or her in the study of the appropriate materials for the next session.

O Complete your copy of "Evaluating Each Session." If you have an apprentice, fill in and discuss this worksheet with him or her.

O Discuss with your supervisor or your apprentice the dynamics of the group process.

O Read "Before the Session" for Group Session 4. Carefully complete all the activities in the member's book for unit 4 if you are ready to move to that unit. If you are using a multiple sessions per unit format, review the materials for Group Session 3 to prepare for your next group.

Out of the Darkness into the Light

Session Goal: Group members will-
- begin to assign to the person who abused them the responsibility for the abuse;
- confront their denial that the abuse had an impact on their lives;
- begin to feel the losses associated with the abuse;
- begin to talk about their feelings;
- become willing to give themselves permission and time to heal.

What to Expect

Some of your group members are beginning to move into stage two. They are beginning to risk trusting this process. They wonder if the group process really is going to meet their goals. Because they are beginning to trust, they are becoming more honest. You will hear more impatience and more complaints about the process, the material, anything to relieve the anxiety and to remove the group focus from the issue at hand-support and recovery from sexual abuse. You may lose some group members at this time. Others will begin to really get to know each other and risk disclosing more about themselves. The overall anxiety level of the group will begin to increase, as the group begins to consider actually working on the tough issues at hand.

At this stage you may be getting a barrage of feelings ranging from sadness to rage. Some of your group members may be realizing for the first time that what happened to them was a criminal act. Others will be validating experiences that they have been discounting for years. Watch for overwhelming emotions to emerge. Be prepared to provide encouragement. If you have survivors who have been on the journey to recovery longer, they can assist in supporting those that have just begun. Right now recovery may feel like wading through a swamp-impossible and not worth the effort. You will have to provide the encouragement and vision that recovery does happen and that it is worth the journey.

Some of your group members may be feeling overwhelmed. The following list contains several ways to help them deal with these feelings.
- Remind them of the plan they developed in unit 1 for managing a crisis.

- Encourage them to set up a regular prayer time with one of their support people.
- Remind them to write their feelings in their journal.
- Encourage them to see their counselor or therapist more often or at least make a telephone contact between sessions.
- Reinforce the need to talk to supportive family members about their journey.
- Remind them that the group is an option for them and that you will support dropping out if the feelings are too intense. Make that decision together with them. Do not coerce, shame, or manipulate someone into staying in group. Simply allow them to graciously exit. The time may not be right.
- Don't make promises for support that you cannot maintain over the long haul. It is unfair to you and to your group member.

Skill Development

Review the skill development section from Group Session 3. Remember to be a mirror for your group members rather than an interpreter of their experiences. When a group member shares an experience or a problem, ask members *what* they felt while this person was sharing, not *how* they were feeling. If you ask *how* you might get "fine." When you ask "what feeling," you cause the person to reach inside and name a feeling they are experiencing rather than a general state.

At this point you will need to focus on your own support system. The task of leading this group can be overwhelming. The needs are overwhelming. Find something else to do that you enjoy. Sing in the choir. Take piano lessons. Plant some daisies. Join the nearest gym. More importantly, increase your prayer time and tell somebody what is going on with you.

You need to remember to maintain healthy boundaries. Do not become enmeshed in your group members lives. If you do, the agenda of the group will become your own codependency rather than recovery for your group members. If you find that you are spending most of your waking moments thinking and talking about your support group, seek some help. Talk to your supervisor or support person about this problem. You might want to read *Untangling Relationships: A*

Christian Perspective on Codependency (item number 7202-73), especially unit 3, "A Warped Sense of Responsibility," to help you learn how to support others without losing yourself in the process.

Before the Session

O Read and complete the learning activities for unit 4 in the member's book.

O Have a flip chart and markers available for use during the session.

O Prepare Scripture/Affirmation cards for unit 5.

O Check room arrangement.

O Provide several boxes of tissues.

During the Session

Arrival-Greet everyone by name. Start on time.

Checking In-
* Ask someone to read the Welcome Statement.
* Ask for someone to share something related to their recovery that they believe is evidence of growth or insight.
* Ask for comments on last week's session.

Share Time-
Introduce the share time with the following analogy. *Denial or discounting sexual abuse is like living in a dark room with a snake. If 1 keep the room dark, 1 can pretend it isn't there. I may think I am safer if I can't see it, but in reality I am not. It also seems a little strange to walk on top of tables, chairs, and cabinets to keep away from something that I am pretending isn't there, but at least 1 don't have to look at it. I have learned to listen very closely to the slightest movement of the snake and to react quickly to get out of its way. It doesn't matter that occasionally I hit the corner of the table and bruise myself or that I have lost my capacity to stand up as long as I don't have to see the snake.*

Very few victims of sexual abuse were abused by a stranger. Most victims have difficulty placing full responsibility for the abuse on the abuser. Victims have difficulty actually saying that the person committed an evil, sinful, and criminal act.
* Ask: *Have you considered yourself a victim of a crime?*
* Listen to their answers. Watch for rationalizations such as, "I was drunk," "I shouldn't have gone in his apartment," "I enjoyed sitting in his lap," or "I wanted him to hold me."

State: *Even if the victim in some way benefits, sexual abuse is sexual abuse. How is this statement true?* Wait for a response. *Are there exceptions?* Read and discuss Sherry's story (page 56).
* Ask if anyone is willing to share how they benefited from the relationship with their perpetrator. After they have finished sharing ask them to repeat after you, *But, I was not responsible for the sexual abuse.*
* The key to healing is to assign responsibility for the abuse to the person who committed the abuse. It was the perpetrator's sin.

Remind your group members that they may also carry some intense feelings about significant others in their world at the time of the abuse. A co-perpetrator's behavior may have also violated the victim's values, beliefs, image, and reality of the world.
* For example, mothers protect their daughters from harm, parents are to take care of their kids. The fact that this person did not or was not able to function according to the victim's values and beliefs results in feelings of betrayal and loss.
* Survivors need to talk about this person's role. Do not discount victims' feelings about the co-perpetrators. Explanations may exist for why this person did not protect, but those explanations do not remove the victims' need for protection or the victims' feelings about the protection they did not receive.
* Victims cannot move to forgiveness or understanding of the co-perpetrator's role without working through the feelings of betrayal, abandonment, and anger.

If you rescue victims by trying to spare their feelings, or if you rescue the co-perpetrators by defending their actions, you will trap the victims in their feelings. If the co-perpetrators are important to them, victims will work through their feelings and losses and create what they want and need in the relationship. Trust the process.

Provide a blank sheet of paper for each group member. Ask group members to write the name of a co-perpetrator. Under that name ask them to write one word that describes how they feel when they think of this person.
* Ask: *Who would like to share what they wrote with the group?* Encourage further sharing of names and feelings. Block any attempts to protect each other from these feelings.
* Ask group members to write the feelings they have identified. Have the group members write the name or role of the person(s) that they connect with those feelings. Look for some repetitions such as mother, God, another sibling, etc.
* Discuss the feelings they may be experiencing as they do this exercise. What feelings did or do they have toward God about the abuse?

Ask: *How did you respond to the request in the text to identify any barriers, especially beliefs or ideas, that keep you from reaching out to God for help in your recovery?* *(page 62)*

Say: *The trauma of sexual abuse also contradicts some of our values, beliefs, and images of God. We sometimes have difficulty realizing that we can't go back to the garden of Eden. We want to believe that God will protect us from all evil and that if He doesn't, I must be responsible, bad, or worthless. Working through the spiritual questions and losses is difficult. We must help each other, listen to each other, and allow each other to be where we are on our journey. We must also remember that God is big enough to let us feel whatever we need to feel.*

Ask someone to read the 23rd Psalm. Ask: *How has God been your shepherd?* If you are leading multiple sessions, encourage your group members to rewrite the 23rd Psalm using their own issues. Refer to the 23rd Psalm (page 70) and to "Survivor's Psalm" (page 71) as examples.

Read the memory verse: Psalm 42:16b. Ask for feelings about this passage. Say the verse together.

Say the unit affirmation together.

I am worthy to have God lead me and comfort me.

Close with a circle of prayer. End with the "Serenity Prayer."

After the Session

O Pray for each member specifically. Pray for group members with special needs.

O Call each group member, encourage him or her in the study of the appropriate materials for the next session.

O Use your copy of "Evaluating Each Session" for this session. If you have an apprentice, fill in and discuss this worksheet with him or her.

O Discuss with your supervisor or your apprentice the dynamics of the group process.

O Read "Before the Session" for Group Session 5. Carefully complete all the activities in the member's book for unit 5 if you are ready to move to that unit. If you are using a multiple sessions per unit format, review the materials for Group Session 4 to prepare for your next group.

The Family in the Storm

Session G o al: Group members will develop an understanding of the effect the rules and roles in a family have on the experience of and recovery from sexual abuse.

What to Expect

The group probably is in transition between stages two and three. The members may be exhibiting some goal-oriented behaviors. Some members may be feeling for the first time in their lives that they can be heard. Some will feel intense grief. Some may experience anxiety and panic because they are giving away their secret. They may also feel accepted, encouraged, determined, and connected. You may begin to see a willingness to allow the intense feelings to emerge and to express the internal and family conflicts created by the recovery journey. By this time members are beginning to feel committed to the task and to each other. You will see them begin to risk encouraging each other to go on.

Skill Development

Group members need to have consistency in group format, but they also need to know that room exists for creativity in the group. This session includes an exercise that will give members an opportunity to risk a bit more. The exercise will help members show more trust in front of the group without calling attention to that fact. The exercise asks members to stand under a sign that describes their role in their family of origin. By physically locating themselves under a sign, some group members may feel a bit exposed. The exercise seems like a simple thing to do, but in a sexual abuse group it is not. If someone refuses, praise her for being able to establish boundaries, and allow her to choose not to participate. It may be the only time in her life that she has had the courage to say no!

As the exercise develops, it will also help your members to identify how the same roles they played in the family are present in group interaction (the family you have created for recovery). You want members to see themselves. They can recognize what they are doing to feel safe in this group of people. Then they can decide if they really need to continue the behavior.

Before the Session

  O Read and complete the learning activities in unit 5 of the member's book.
  O Have a flip chart and markers available for use during the session.
  O Prepare Scripture/Affirmation cards for unit 6.
  O Contact group members to encourage them and address any fears, reservations, and expectations.
  O Provide several boxes of tissues.
  O Make a poster of the characteristics of a dysfunctional family (page 75).
  O Make paper strips with large letters identifying the roles in dysfunctional families (Scapegoat, Hero, Surrogate Spouse, Lost Child, Surrogate Parent, and Clown (page 82).
  O Place the strips around the room but cover them so they cannot be read.

During the Session

Arrival-Greet everyone by name. Start on time.

Checking In-
• Ask someone to read the Welcome Statement.
• Ask for any comments or questions on last week's session.
• Ask if anyone would like to read their rewrite of the 23rd Psalm if you have chosen this project.

Share Time-
In recovery from any kind of abuse, we need a clear understanding of the role and function of the family. That is especially true with recovery from sexual abuse. Both past and present family issues tremendously affect sexual abuse recovery.

The impact of the family is present even for the victim of stranger rape. We can see that an assault has an impact on the way the victim responds to normal family interactions. The way the family members respond to the rape affects the way victims view themselves and affects the recovery. For example, a husband may react negatively to having sex with the rape victim. She feels rejected because she doesn't understand that he is not rejecting her but rather the intensity of his anger and fear over the rape.

Display the poster of the characteristics of a dysfunctional family (page 75). As you review the list of characteristics, discuss how each one relates to the experience of your group members.

- Ask group members to identify how the characteristics describe their family of origin.
- Lead by giving several examples from your own experience. The following is an example of a surrogate parent: In a family with an alcoholic father a child may become the confidant and emotional support for the mother. In taking that role, the child sacrifices his emotional needs to take care of those of a parent. If the alcoholic father is also sexually abusive, the child would have to violate his role in the family in order to tell the mother about the abuse.
- Ask: *Do these characteristics describe your family today?*
- *How do you think this affects your recovery?*
- *What would you like to do to begin to change these areas of dysfunction?*

Ask for feelings from your group: Expect anything. Some of your group members may feel enlightened. Others may be confused. Some may not be able to identify any feeling.

Remind your group members that families change slowly. Your group members need to realize that unless they are in danger this is not the time to make major decisions about the family. Allow the process to work. Encourage them to set small goals and to maintain them consistently. For example, don't expect to tell your spouse, "Our family is closed to the outside world so we need to entertain two nights a week." Instead, find a couple and go out to a movie and have them over for dessert sometime this month. Do something similar again next month, and the next. Stay focused and continue to move forward but with consistent and realistic goals.

Shelter from the Storm describes the roles children develop in dysfunctional families. These roles are either assigned or unconsciously chosen by the child. They are called survival roles because they are in fact the position in the family that best allowed the child to survive the trauma of the family dysfunction.

- Walk around the room; uncover and read the strips you have posted.
- Ask your group members to choose a role they played in their family of origin and to stand under that role. They may have played others, but ask them to choose the one they most identify with.
- Ask each person to share how they played that role and the effect it had upon their sexual abuse

and/or the effect it had on how they coped with it. If they were abused as an adult, this role affected how they have coped with that abuse as well.

- Ask the group members to consider how they may be playing those same roles in the current family or in this group. How do they use those behaviors to survive the pain of the abuse or other uncomfortable and abusive situations.?
- Do a feelings check. Ask: *What are you feeling after talking about your family role(s)? Sadness? Anger? Loneliness? Fear? Shame? Guilt? Other?*

Survivors of sexual abuse have a difficult time letting go of the feeling of responsibility for the abuse. Fantasy bonding is one explanation for this difficulty. Fantasy bonding means the victims create a fantasy relationship to the abuser or to a family member who could have protected them. They rationalize, make excuses, and sometimes even recreate this person rather than face the reality that the person was responsible for the abuse.

- Ask your group members if they would be willing to share what they wrote about fantasy bonding (page 83).
- Describe any fantasy bonding you may have with family members.

Many survivors keep their abuse a secret to protect the family from having to deal with the fact that the abuse is occurring or has occurred. Sometimes they keep the secret because the victim is afraid that someone will get hurt physically or emotionally or that the family will not survive. The victim will endure the pain of the abuse rather than risk losing the family.

The risk or fear of losing the family is also present in recovery from sexual abuse. Deciding who to tell and how much to tell is a big step for the survivor and should not be rushed into prematurely. The family usually does not welcome the survivor with open arms when their secret is revealed. The survivor's strength and expectations should be the first consideration. The support group facilitator or group should not design, encourage, or push for the survivor to reveal the secret. This decision belongs to the survivor and should be made with a therapist and therapeutic support. Block any moves on the part of other group members to pressure a peer into a confrontation with the family. We will address confrontation much deeper in the study. At this time you need to prevent premature action. Even if the perpetrator is a non-family member, it is important to allow the survivor the right to decide without pressure and coercion when and how to reveal the abuse. Allow the survivor to identify and talk about how and what they did to protect the family.

- Ask your group members to share what they feel about the role of their family of origin in their recovery.
- Ask them how they responded to the following question in the members book (page 87): *If your family chooses not to pursue recovery from dysfunctional behavior, how might this decision affect your recovery? Your future?*

Childhood Pictures Assignment-

If you are using a multiple sessions format, invite your group members to bring childhood pictures of themselves to next week's session. You may want to ask them to bring pictures of other significant family members to share with the group and to talk about their relationship with one or two significant people. For instance, you may want to ask them to share the picture of a person who was a significant source of strength or comfort. Avoid asking for pictures of the perpetrator. If someone brings such a picture on their own, accept it and process their feelings. After you have finished looking at the pictures and sharing, continue with the following suggestions for the session as time permits.

Discuss whether your group is a functional family. Ask members to share their response to the learning activity on page 88 in the member's book Ask them to describe a safe place.

After they have described a safe place, ask them if the *Shelter from the Storm* group feels like a safe place. Ask group members to be honest with themselves and each other. Conflict can be resolved in functional families. It is not ignored. This is a time for you to make sure you choose to not take any response personally. The members may need to test you and others in the group to see if they can indeed say that they are not feeling safe. Maybe they are afraid someone is not really listening to them, or they are afraid they are not being accepted. These feelings need to be communicated. Accept each comment, whether positive or negative, without criticism or defense.

Thank each member for their input. State that this may be the most difficult thing you do as a group. The only thing harder to talk about than the sexual abuse will be the ongoing relationship issues in your group. They are to be commended for being willing to share with one another at that level.

Read the story of Tamar in 2 Samuel 13:1-20 and ask your group to respond to this biblical account of sexual abuse. Remind your group members that sexual abuse is not a new problem and that God did not think He

needed to keep it a secret. Here it is in King David's family! In the lineage of Christ! I think God wants us to know that we don't have to hide and pretend it didn't happen. Even though Tamar remained silent and desolate in Absalom's house, God told her story to the whole world. In His family we can talk about it! He knew she was innocent. He knew she was clean.

Say the unit affirmation together.

I am Clean!

Say Isaiah 54:4 to your group:

God's message and promise to you is: Do not be afraid; you will not suffer shame. Do not fear disgrace; you will not be humiliated. You will forget the shame of your youth.

-Isaiah 54:4

Say: *Unit 6 addresses the issue of shame. In that unit you will have the opportunity to write a sexual abuse incident. I will be praying for you this week as you address this issue.*

Close with a circle of prayer. End with the "Serenity Prayer."

After the Session

O Pray for each member specifically. Pray for group members with special needs.

O Call each group member, encourage him or her in the study of the appropriate materials for the next session.

O Use your copy of "Evaluating Each Session" this session. If you have an apprentice, fill in and discuss this worksheet with him or her.

O Discuss with your supervisor or your apprentice the dynamics of the group process.

O Read "Before the Session" for Group Session 6. Carefully complete all the activities in the member's book for unit 6 if you are ready to move to that unit. If you are planning to continue working in this unit, review the materials for Group Session 5 to prepare for your next group.

Letting Go of Shame and Guilt

Session Goal: Group members will-
- identify the feelings of shame and guilt;
- begin to recognize that isolation and withdrawal are outward expressions of shame;
- confront the shame by writing about one incident of sexual abuse.

What to Expect

Your group may still be in transition between stages two and three; however, sexual abuse groups easily return to stage one depending on the topic at hand. Shame and guilt can cause members to withdraw and isolate. As they worked in the member's book, group members have been given their first opportunity to write about a sexual abuse incident. This may have generated feelings of guilt, shame, anger, or rage. This exercise probably produced some additional anxiety. They may act out the feelings that are generated by the material. Expect the group to have a difficult time getting started. Be patient. If this is a repeat session, this is a good time to rely on your members who are on their second time around to help lead the way.

Skill Development

In this and following skill development sections, you will find a list of behaviors that may be disruptive or harmful to your group. Evaluate your group for these behaviors.
- Group doesn't stay on task: Sexual abuse groups are notorious for finding ways to avoid talking about sexual abuse. You may have to repeatedly say, "Those things are important, but we are here to talk about sexual abuse. How do these things relate to your abuse?"
- Care-takers: You will find that some of your group members will try to take care of everyone else and avoid talking about their own issues. When that happens, invite that group member to share what they have written in their book in response to a section, or to share what they are feeling about their issues.
- Advice-givers: Some people use advice giving or fixing others to block their own feelings. Explain that we need to support people as they discover the answers for themselves. Ask the one giving advice to share what motivates them to give advice. Often the motivation is care, concern, and love. Ask them to share those feelings instead of the advice.

Before the Session

O Read and complete the learning activities in unit 6 of the member's book.
O Check the room arrangement.
O Have a flip chart and markers available for use during the session.
O Prepare Scripture/Affirmation cards for unit 7.
O Provide several boxes of tissues for the room.

During the Session

Arrival--Greet everyone by name. Start on time.

Checking In-
- Ask someone to read the Welcome Statement.
- Ask for any comments or questions on last week's session.

Share Time-
You want group members to recognize that shame is the result of feeling responsible for the abuse or unworthy of being protected from the abuse. Even though shame is an awful feeling, it serves to protect the victim from other feelings that are more frightening. The survivor would rather feel the shame and blame for the abuse than to face the reality that they had absolutely no control. If victims can see themselves as bad or shameful, therefore responsible, then they can pretend that they were not so vulnerable to the whims of the perpetrator. When survivors drop this illusion of control, then they must accept that their world was unsafe. The adults or authorities that were supposed to make the world safe failed. They may even have to recognize that their life was in danger. They will have to see how horrible the abuse was. They may have to admit that someone they loved did something horrible and awful to them. Shame thus becomes a safe place to hide from the fear and the awful hurt.
- Use the material in the unit to give a mini-lecture on the role of shame in the life of the survivor.

- Ask for questions. Respond with positive reflections. Help group members identify with each other.
- Ask if someone would like to share how they have been shaming themselves for the sexual abuse. What are some of the words and phrases that they use to judge themselves?
- Use the judge imagery to help them to identify the "sentence" they have given themselves.

Ask them to share about their experience of writing, "I am significant. I do count. I am worthwhile." Check to see that they have completed the assignment (page 95-96). Encourage any who have not completed the exercise to do the writing.

Use material from the text to give a mini-lecture on the three major sources of shame messages. Lecturing this material will remove some pressure from the group. They will be more prone to talk if they see you taking charge. Write the three major sources on a tear sheet or marker board-
1. the message of the abuser
2. the message from your own body
3. verbal messages from others

- As you lecture, ask the group members to share the shame messages they experienced under each source. Write them down on the tear sheet as examples. The combined list will enforce group cohesiveness and prevent any one member from being singled out.
- Ask your group what they are feeling about these shame messages right now.
- Ask someone to explain the difference between shame and guilt. Give the group as much time as they need to discuss.
- Explain that shame and guilt are fed and protected by the secrecy surrounding sexual abuse. A large part of healing is breaking through the secrecy and allowing the medicine of love, support, and encouragement to get to the wound caused by the abuse. Be sure that you communicate that you understand how difficult this is to do.

To actually tell someone exactly what happened during the abuse is frightening. We can talk about the fact that we were abused and how we feel about the event, the perpetrator, or the co-perpetrator, and still almost pretend it happened to someone else. When we write about and talk about the actual details, when and where it happened, and how we felt then and there, we take power over the shame and guilt. We have faced the event head-on. It is no longer chasing us. We have caught it and taken power over it. We have also broken through the power of the secret.

Because reading about the actual abuse is so frightening, your group needs to know you have a method for making the exercise safe. The structured process described below-of writing about then reading about an event-provides that safety. This method can be a powerful experience. The method involves writing about a specific instance, then in a safe and affirming environment reading what you have written.
- Before the group member reads, ask her what she is feeling. Tell her to respond with one- or two-word statements-such as sad, angry, hurt, or anxious.
- Tell the group member to read what she has written when she is ready and to read slowly.
- After she has finished reading, ask her again what she is feeling.
- After the reader has shared her feelings, ask the group members what they are feeling. Explain to them that you want only feelings, not descriptions of feeling. Demonstrate by giving feedback first. Say "While you were reading I felt (mad, sad, rage, lonely, paralyzed, etc.) Do not allow other statements such as "That must have been awful," or "You should have kicked him."
- After each group member has shared, ask the reader again what she is feeling. The group member will usually add new feelings by connecting with a feeling shared by another group member. Sometimes she will state feelings such as understood, validated, etc.
- After the group member has shared, ask the group to be a mirror for the reader. What did they see and hear as she was reading? Model this feedback first yourself to teach your group how to do it. You want to say things like. "You sat very still. You began to cry when you read about .... I saw you clinch your fist several times as you came to the end of the reading." Do not interpret why you thought the behaviors occurred, just state what you saw or heard. You will shut down the feelings of the reader if you interpret the experience.
- After others have been a mirror for the reader, ask the reader again for feelings. Take this slowly. Give the reader time to connect with the feelings generated by the feedback.
- After the group member has read an episode of sexual abuse, affirm the reader for a job well done. Ask the reader what the experience was like for him or her.1

Tell your group that this is the process you will use anytime someone has an incident of sexual abuse to share. Writing out the incident and then reading it to the group provides the least vulnerable and most supportive environment possible for sharing this difficult material.

If you are a survivor, you may want to read an incident you have written and ask your co-facilitator to facilitate the feedback or vice versa. This will demonstrate the method and help your group feel safe.

Allow anyone who is ready to read their incident as long as there is time and the group is responding well. Provide encouragement and support.

If no one is ready, be prepared to role-play this with fictitious episodes until the group gets comfortable with hearing details. This is tough work. Tell members they will get it accomplished. Do not coerce anyone to write or read incidents. Some may be more ready to share specific details with the group than others. Accept your members where they are.

Ask your group to share their response to the exercise on the bottom of page 104 and top of 105 in the members book. The exercise contrasts what they have felt about themselves with what the Scriptures say about them. Say: *God is in the process of recreating you into a vessel He can use. He can remove the shame, guilt, fear, and despair caused by the abuse.*

Say the unit affirmation together.

I am wonderfully made.

Repeat the memory verse together.

There is therefore now no condemnation to them which are in Christ Jesus.
                                        -Romans 8:1

Close with a circle of prayer and the "Serenity Prayer."

After the Session

- O Pray for each member specifically. Pray for group members with special needs.
- O Call each group member, encourage him or her in the study of the appropriate materials for the next session.
- O Complete your copy of "Evaluating Each Session." If you have an apprentice, fill in and discuss this worksheet with him or her.
- O Discuss with your supervisor or your apprentice the dynamics of the group process.
- O Read "Before the Session" for Group Session 7 and carefully complete all the activities in the member's book for unit 7 if you are ready to move to that unit. If you are using a multiple ses-

sions per unit format, review the materials for Group Session 6 to prepare for your next group.

Notes

[1] This structured process is adapted from Jesse Collins and Nancy Carson, *Trauma Resolution Therapy: A Structured Psychodynamic Approach to the Treatment of Post-traumatic Stress, TRT Book One*, (Collins & Carson, 1989).

Feeling the Anger and Hurt

Session Goal: Group members will-
- learn that anger and hurt are appropriate, acceptable, and necessary emotions in recovery from sexual abuse;
- discover that they can feel anger and hurt without negative consequences.

What to Expect

Your group will be developing some deep relationships by this time. Members have really begun to trust each other, or they have dropped out. If you have some members that have begun to share specifics about their abuse, they may be experiencing an increased level of anxiety-feeling exposed and vulnerable. You may want to remind them that this is about breaking the family rules of "don't trust, don't feel, and don't talk about it." Group members may feel hesitant to address the anger and hurt they feel toward the perpetrators and co-perpetrators. Many of your group members may be afraid to feel anger. They may have been taught by their parents that anger is a sin. Some may have developed the mistaken belief that the Bible teaches that anger is a sin.

Skill Development

Review the following list of disruptive or harmful behaviors.
- The domineering group member: If a group member consistently takes over the group, be positively assertive with the group. Say things like: "We need to hear what others in the group feel about that." or "Thank you for sharing. Now let me hear from someone else."
- The consistently quiet group member: Occasionally you will have a member who comes to group and rarely or never says a word. If you allow this to happen, the others in the group will begin to resent this person's lack of involvement, plus it will become more and more difficult for this person to respond. Function as a gatekeeper for this person. Ask him directly to share what he is thinking or feeling. Look for body language that indicates that he is responding to someone or something in the group. Even a slight smile, or a different tilt of the head can indicate emotional contact.

- The member who interrupts others: You can address this by simply holding up your hand in front of you and stating, "Excuse me, Sue has not finished," or "Sue was still speaking." Address the person's issue after Sue has finished.

Since you will be talking about anger in this unit, you may find your group members disagreeing with one another about the appropriate role and use of anger in recovery. Be careful not to make moral judgments about the disagreements. Redirect your group members and explore with them the source of their beliefs about anger.

Before the Session

O Read and complete the learning activities in unit 7 of the member's book.
0 Check room arrangement.
O Prepare Scripture/Affirmation cards for unit 8.
O Provide several boxes of tissues.
O Prepare the Thermometer poster that represents degrees of anger. Draw a thermometer. Toward the bottom write the word, "Irritated;" in the middle write, "Angry;" close to the top of the thermometer write the word, "Furious." Include a few marks between each word on the thermometer so group members may express their degree of anger.
O Prepare a poster listing the three choices we have about anger (page 116).
O Make copies of the Feeling Facts handout found on page 63 of this guide.

During the Session

Arrival-
- Greet everyone by name.
- Distribute paper and markers/pens to everyone.
- Start on time.

Checking In-
- Ask someone to read the Welcome Statement.
- Ask for any comments or questions on last week's session.

Share Time-

Anger is an important emotion. The memory verse for this unit includes the imperative, "Be angry." One might ask the question, "Why would the Bible give such an instruction?" Anger is a danger sign. To ignore anger is similar to ignoring the "check engine" light on your car. If you let it go long enough, something is going to fall apart! Anger tells us that something is wrong. It is saying to sexual abuse victims that someone has hurt them. It says that their needs and wants must be considered. It says that their values and beliefs have been violated. Once survivors begin to realize it was not their fault-"I am not to blame!" "I was molested!" "I was raped!"-anger and rage begin to emerge.

Sometimes survivors first find it easier to feel angry about what happened to another group member. As they support the anger of that group member, their own begins to bubble to the surface. The anger may explode like the erupting of a volcano. It is normal for the survivor to feel overwhelmed and overpowered by the intensity of the feelings at times. Encourage your group members to make use of their support people when they feel overwhelmed. They each need a couple of people who can listen to them rant and rave if necessary.

Put up the Thermometer poster you prepared prior to the session.
- Ask group members to write their names on the thermometer at the level they believe represents their anger about the sexual abuse.
- After group members have written their names, lead the group in a discussion about their choices.
- Be careful to ask for what they feel when they look at where they appear on the thermometer. What is helpful about their position? What is not helpful? What do they need to do now to increase their strength and hope in their recovery?

Now draw a volcano on a tear sheet. Use this to communicate the role of anger and anxiety in the management of other feelings. Explain that the volcano provides a picture of our treatment of anger. The inside of the volcano contains feelings related to the abuse. The outside of the volcano is made of anxiety. Anytime survivors get close to the volcano, they feel the anxiety. They expect a massive explosion. Usually they fear anger most. People usually begin to feel anger when they reject the false beliefs about the abuse.

Once survivors can feel angry, they can then feel hurt, fear, guilt, sadness, shame, loneliness, rejection, and abandonment. The feelings lose their power when the survivor faces them and deals with them.

- Say: *Each of us in some way carries a mental picture of how or where we stuff our feelings . Some of you may identify with the volcano. Others may not. I would like to ask each of you to draw a picture that shows what you do with feelings.* If your group has a difficult time with this, you might share another example with them . One survivor drew a box . The walls of the box are made of anxiety. The lid was anger. Inside it held lots of little boxes named fear, hate, guilt, numbness, etc. Give them plenty of time to do this. Ask them to share their drawing with the group.

Distribute the Feeling Facts handout. Read through it with the group. Discuss how it relates specifically to the feeling of anger and the expression of anger and rage.

Refer to the poster you made before the session listing the three choices we have about anger.
1. We can turn it to the outside and blame others for all the bad things that have happened to us.
2. We can turn it inside and blame ourselves for the bad things that have happened to us. (Either of these two choices will eventually lead to emotional destruction.)
3. We can learn to express our anger as a God-given emotion.

- Ask your group members to share what they typically do with anger.
- Share how you learned to express your anger appropriately.
- Share some examples of ways of dealing with intense anger. To the list below add any other methods that you have found helpful.
  - Tearing up a phone book. With each page state a reason for your anger.
  - Prayer. Tell God about your anger. He gets angry too. Remember Jesus drove the money changers out of the temple.
  - Exercise.
  - Screaming.
  - Hitting/throwing a tennis ball.
  - Making a list. I am angry at you because ...
- Sometimes we use anger to run away from emotionally intense situations.
- Anger can be the indication of a deeper emotion. Encourage your group members to state their anger. "I feel angry" or I feel angry with _____ because_____"

Read this excerpt from *Shelter: "I used to think that I needed God magically to take away all my emotional pain. Sometimes I still wish that could be true, but what I really need to know is that God doesn't see me as damaged goods.*

God hears me when I en; and shares my anger about the unfairness and injustice over what happened to me. God loved me before the abuse happened, during the abuse, and will love me forever."

Refer to the following exercise from page 124 of the member's book. "Write a brief statement telling God about your anger at your abuse and thanking God for being angry too. Thank God for loving you before, during, and after the abuse." Ask if anyone would like to share their statement with the group. Allow for discussion of their feelings about God.

Quote your memory verse together.

Be angry, and yet do not sin.
-Ephesians 4:26, NASB

Quote your unit affirmation together.

I have permission to feel angry and hurt.

Close with a circle of prayer. End with the "Serenity Prayer."

After the Session

- **0** Pray for each member specifically. Pray for group members with special needs.
- **0** Call each group member. Encourage him or her in the study of the appropriate materials for the next session.
- **0** Use your copy of "Evaluating Each Session" this session. If you have an apprentice, fill in and discuss this worksheet with him or her.
- **0** Discuss with your supervisor or your apprentice the dynamics of the group process.
- **0** Read "Before the Session" for Group Session 8 and carefully complete all the activities in the member's book for unit 8 if you are ready to move to that unit. If you are using a multiple sessions per unit format, review the materials for Group Session 7 to prepare for your next group.

Healing Loneliness and Fear

Session Goal: Group members will-
- recognize that for survivors of sexual abuse to feel loneliness and fear is normal;
- begin to distinguish between healthy and unhealthy methods of compensating for fear and loneliness.

What to Expect

Two of the most devastating feelings experienced by the sexual abuse survivor are loneliness and fear. These two feelings become intertwined. They feel loneline s and the fear of being alone, yet they also experience the fear of being exposed, of being seen, of not being alone. This circular pattern is one of the most difficult problems for the survivor to confront.

The group process itself is one of the best ways to confront this cycle. Your group members have begun to develop relationships with one another. They have listened to each other's stories, issues, and problems. They have shared their secrets with one another. In essence they are not alone anymore; however, this frightens them. This self-exposure creates fear and anxiety. This unit may cause your group members to identify and experience the feeling of being exposed. They may react in many different ways. Some may shut down and be afraid to talk about this subject. Some may clown or otherwise act out to avoid the subject. Others may be excited to realize they are finally making some emotional connections. Accept whatever they present without judgment or interpretation.

Skill Development

Evaluate your group for these behaviors.
- Joking around or lack of seriousness: Occasionally you will have a session when several group members are feeling particularly upbeat. Some may use this to avoid feeling the pain. You may have a session when a couple of group members are simply on top of things. Point out the differences between the emotional messages of various members. Point out that we are individuals and that group members can be at different places emotionally; however, do not let a group member take another group member's issues with less seriousness than they deserve. Simply point out that you see them having a difficult time connecting with the feelings of the group member. Ask: "I wonder why you find it hard to empathize with _____?"
- Tension in the group: There will be times when tension will exist in the group, and you may not know why. Maybe the group is extra quiet or there is little eye contact. Simply state your feeling, "There seems to be some tension in the group tonight. Would someone share why they think that is so?" If it becomes clear that the tension is about an issue between members of a subgroup that has formed in the group, acknowledge that you need to discuss the issue with them privately. Schedule a time to do so. At that time you will need to determine what you will share with the larger group when you meet again.
- Displaced anger: As your group members get in touch with their feelings, they may not know how to express them appropriately. Sarcasm is often a method to express displaced anger. If a group member is sarcastic, you may want to give them feelings feedback about the sarcasm. "When you speak to me that way I feel · however, I am also wondering what you are feeling. I am willing to hear it." If this doesn't work, meet with this person privately to encourage identification of the hurt that is underneath the sarcasm.

Before the Session

O Read and complete the learning activities in unit 8 of the member's book.
0 Check the room arrangement.
O Have a flip chart and markers available for use during the session.
O Prepare Scripture/Affirmation cards for unit 9.
O Provide several boxes of tissues.
O Prepare posters as needed for any activity you choose to utilize.

During the Session

Arrival-Greet everyone by name. Start on time.

Checking In-
- Open with a short prayer.
- Ask someone to read the Welcome Statement.
- Ask if anyone would like to share what they have done to get in touch with and express their anger during the week.

Share Time-
Say: *Loneliness and fear are common feelings for survivors of sexual abuse. For survivors to begin to shut themselves away emotionally and sometimes physically is normal because they have been hurt, and the world no longer feels like a safe place. When something hurts you, to be afraid of that source of pain is normal. However, the fear and isolation begin to create more fear and loneliness-feelings that are unrelated to the original abuse.*

- The goal for the survivor is to feel the fear and loneliness related to the abuse and to identify and let go of unrelated fear and loneliness.
- Give examples from your own experience.
- Invite your group members to talk about how loneliness and fear have been a part of their lives.

Ask your group members to name the things that the sexual abuse victim might be afraid of. These may or may not be a part of their personal experience. Record these on a tear sheet. Your list should include items such as-

Fear of the perpetrator
Fear of abandonment
Fear of the unknown
Fear of harm
Fear of rejection

Help members to recognize that they can feel the fear, but that they do not have to stay in the fear. Help them to see that they can experience strength and hope. Ask them to refer to the member's book as a resource to address these fears.

Ask members to refer to the work they have done in the member's book this week and to share something that was especially important or meaningful to them.

Ask your group members to share how they responded to the exercise on page 134 that asked them to circle the actions they use to run away from their fears. After they have shared their responses, ask for any items they may have added. Then ask: *What would you like to change about your lists?*

- Lead the group as you pray about the changes members want to make. Ask God to give you the courage to begin today to set small goals for yourself in at least one area.

- Ask if they would like to share one of their goals.

Say: *There is hope for restoration from loneliness and fear; however, it requires that we recognize how we are involved in the process of holding on to the loneliness and fear.*

Refer your group to the series of exercises on page 137 that begins: "Write a list of your thought statements that cause you to feel lonely. Beside each statement describe the feeling it brings. These thoughts usually are false beliefs that keep us in bondage to the loneliness." On a tear sheet write one example of your work with this exercise. Ask a group member to share an example of their work with this exercise. Record it on the tear sheet. Your tear sheet should look like this:

Feeling_____

Thought Statement _____

_____

Rewrite _____

_____

Ask members to share their feelings about this exercise.

Ask your group to refer to the following exercise from page 138.

> Review your list of fears from lesson 3. Do your fears protect or serve you in any way?
> O Yes O No If so, explain.

Ask them to share their reactions to the exercise. Be prepared for some anger and resistance. Accept it with grace and understanding. Say that you realize it is difficult work and that it may seem impossible. After the members that want to share this exercise have done so, move on to the work in lesson five.

Use the material in lesson 5 to share with your group about the spiritual journey of resolution and restoration. You may want to give a mini-lecture. You may want to ask them to volunteer to share their responses to the material. Help members to connect with the love that God has for them and with the fact that He has always loved them.

Quote your memory verse together.
Even though I walk through the valley of the shadow of death, I will fear no evil, for you are with me; your rod and staff, they comfort me.

-Psalm 23:4

Quote your unit affirmation together.
In Christ I am never alone.

Close with a circle of prayer. End with the "Serenity Prayer."

After the Session

O Pray for each member specifically. Pray especially for group members with special needs.

O Call each group member. Encourage him or her in the study of the appropriate materials for the next session.

O Use your copy of "Evaluating Each Session." If you have an apprentice, fill in and discuss this worksheet with him or her.

O Discuss with your supervisor or your apprentice the dynamics of the group process.

O Read "Before the Session" for Group Session 9 and carefully complete all the activities in the member's book for unit 9 if you are ready to move to that unit. If you are using a multiple sessions per unit format, review the materials for Group Session 8 to prepare for your next group.

Beginning to Trust Again

Session Goal: Group members will—
- define trust and determine individuals in their life whom they can trust;
- discover how they have used control to feel safe and secure;
- begin to replace nonproductive attempts at control with productive ones;
- learn to use the "Serenity Prayer" to help them gain control over their feelings, thoughts, and actions.

What to Expect

The content of this unit may cause your group members to identify some trust issues within the group. For the first time in some of the member's lives, they will have permission to tell someone that they are having trouble trusting that person. Allowing your group members to affirm or confront one another can be a healthy experience. Clarify any false or unrealistic relationship expectations and affirm those that are realistic.

Expect one or two of your group members to be especially interested in using the "Serenity Prayer" as a method for organizing their recovery issues. The exercises in the unit present an especially helpful method for separating the issues that are outside of our personal control from those that are within our control.

Skill Development

Evaluate your group for these behaviors.
- Argumentative group members: You may find that group members will struggle with the issues of trust and control. They may have a difficult time believing that the need to control others or the inability to prevent others from controlling them is related to their recovery from sexual abuse. If group members argue with one another about this, point out that their need for others to agree with them is an example of control!

- Everyone talking at one time: Remind group members that they need to value the time and issues of the other person. Do not allow the group to become chaotic and out of control. They need to trust each other to allow each person time to communicate freely.

Review your active listening skills. Listen for the meaning behind the words. To clarify your assumptions, ask, "What do you mean?"

Remember to maintain eye contact. Sit facing the person who is speaking; lean forward slightly. Listen for thoughts, feelings, attitudes, opinions, and perceptions. Remember, feeling statements begin "I feel_____
When a thought is expressed, ask for the feeling that is connected to it.

Before the Session

O Read and complete the learning activities in unit 9 of the member's book.
O Have a flip chart and markers available for use during the session.
O Prepare Scripture/Affirmation cards for unit 10.
O Provide several boxes of tissues.
O Prepare a poster with the following fill-in-the-blank sentences:

_____ is the road to recovery!
_____ blocks faith.
I need_____

O Make four posters outlining the parts of the "Serenity Prayer."
1) God,
2) Grant me the serenity to accept the things I cannot change.
3) Grant me the courage to change the things I can.
4) Grant me the wisdom to know the difference.
O Provide one three-by-five-inch card for each group member.

During the Session

Arrival-Greet everyone by name. Start on time.

Checking In-
- Ask someone to read the Welcome Statement.
- Ask if anyone has written a sexual abuse incident they would like to read.

Share Time-

Survivors of sexual abuse tend to experience trust as an ali-or-nothing issue. They bounce back and forth from trusting everyone to trusting no one. They shift back and forth between brick walls and chain-link fences. This uncertainty creates such a feeling of desperation that survivors ultimately decide that people really aren't trustworthy, and that to never trust again is the only way to be safe.

Help your group take small steps in trusting others. First help them to develop realistic expectations of others. To teach them to have realistic boundaries, you as facilitator must practice clear and realistic boundaries. Your group members need to know that trust is earned in a relationship. The people who abused them violated their trust. Others in their world will too. In fact, none of us can be completely trustworthy. All of us make mistakes and let others down at times, but the violation from sexual abuse cannot be discounted as making a mistake or letting someone down. Survivors feel all breaches in trust with an intensity similar to that of the sexual abuse. They need to trust a little at a time to rewrite this script and diminish this effect.

To begin your share time, ask group members to turn to page 144. Ask someone to read Jeanie's story that begins at the bottom of the page.

- Members were to underline the people in the story who violated Jeanie's trust. Ask them to share who they underlined and why.
- Discuss the feedback paragraph from page 145: "One person underlined *mother, stepdad, uncles, brothers, ex-husbands.* Then she realized that she needed to underline Jeanie's name also. Like other survivors, Jeanie realized that her ability to make wise decisions about relationships had been damaged. She did not know how to make wise decisions about people. She could not recognize a person who would abuse her. Jeanie needed guidelines to help her rebuild her own ability to tell safe people from abusive people."

Explain that, because of our inability to identify trustworthy people, we continue to victimize ourselves.

- Ask group members to describe the person they listed as a safe, healthy person (page 145).
- On a tear sheet, record the responses your group gave to this part of the exercise.
- From the group responses and your own additions. Compile a list of guidelines to help you determine if someone or something is trustworthy.

Divide your group into two smaller groups. Give each group a tear sheet titled "Hopes and Expectations in Relationships."

- Ask each group to record what they hope and expect from a relationship.
- After they have finished, ask each group to share their sheet with the other group. You will find your group discussing issues such as level of openness, time, energy, care, and concern.
- Ask: *What do hopes and expectations have to do with trust?*

Discuss realistic versus unrealistic expectations of others and of ourselves. Many of the symptoms of co-dependency center around unrealistic expectations of ourselves and others. These expectations are issues of trust and control. You may want to encourage your group members to consider participating in both an *Untangling Relationships* discovery group and a *Conquering Codependency* support group after they have finished *Shelter from the Storm.*

Ask your group members to share how they responded to the following exercise (page 147).

Check the description that best describes your response to God at this time in your recovery.
O I shut myself off from God.
O I recognize God's presence.
O I doubt that God exists.
O I am disappointed by my inability to trust God.
O I am waiting for God to give me an unmistakable sign.
O other_____

Share your response with your group. Remind them to be honest with themselves and the group. There are no wrong answers. The important thing is to identify where they are on the journey, not to focus on where they think they "should" be. Allow plenty of time for discussion and sharing.

Ask if anyone would like to share their list of people they can trust. Maybe someone would like to read one of the letters they wrote in response to the assignment in the text (page 148). If you have observed group members learning to trust one another, this may be a good time to point that out and to affirm them for their growth. If it is appropriate, you might ask members to tell one another how they have seen one another grow in their ability to trust.

Say: *One of the primary losses experienced as a result of sexual abuse is safety and security. The survivor attempts to control to restore that safety and security.*

- Deliver a mini-lecture on the section entitled "Learning True Control" (page 150), or you may read the folJr paragraphs under that heading.

Put up the poster with the fill-in-the-blank sentences. Fill in the blanks as your group responds.

Learning to trust is the road to recovery!
Control blocks faith.
I need people.

Say: *Sometimes our need for control effects our relationships with other people.* Ask your group members to share how they responded to the following exercise from page 153.

Describe the effect your need for control has had on your relationships with others.

Say: *You were asked at the close of lesson 3 in this unit to identify one thing or situation in your life where you can safely give up some control. I am going to give you a three-by-five-inch card. I want you to write down on that card that one thing you have chosen to trust to someone else. I want to invite you to give that card to a fellow group member or one of your support people. Ask them to pray that you will be able to accomplish your goal. Next week I will ask for volunteers to share their progress.* After they have written the one thing, you might ask if anyone would like to share with the group. Allow time for discussion and feelings about the exercise. Pray for the group members to accomplish their goals.

Say: *It is important that we learn to trust others and to trust ourselves to be able to determine who is trustworthy.* Ask the group to share any special insights or meaningful experiences they had in lesson 4. Give them time to look over the lesson. If no one responds, be ready with something you have learned from the lesson to get them started.

Uncover the four "Serenity Prayer" tear sheets you prepared prior to the session. Use the material from the member's book to help your group members learn to use this important method in their struggle to learn trust and to develop discernment about the issue of control in their lives. Fill in the posters with possible responses under each heading. Encourage them to use this as a way to organize a prayer journal. Review and discuss with the group pages 158-161.

Quote your memory verse together.
May the God of hope fill you with all joy and peace as you trust in him, so that you may overflow with hope by the power of the Holy Spirit.
-Romans 15:13

Quote your unit affirmation together.
I can trust myself and others.

Close with a circle of prayer. End with the "Serenity Prayer."

After the Session

O Pray for each member specifically. Pray for group members with special needs.

O Call each group member. Encourage him or her in the study of the appropriate materials for the next session.

O Use your copy of "Evaluating Each Session." If you have an apprentice, fill in and discuss this worksheet with him or her.

O Discuss with your supervisor or your apprentice the dynamics of the group process.

O Read "Before the Session" for Group Session 10 and carefully complete all the activities in the member's book for unit 10 if you are ready to move to that unit. If you are using a multiple sessions per unit format, review the materials for Group Session 9 to prepare for your next group.

The Process of Forgiveness

Session Goal: Group members will-
- recognize that forgiving benefits the survivor and refusing to forgive harms the survivor;
- discover that the severity of the offense against them is not diminished because they choose to forgive the person(s) who committed the offense;
- understand that forgiveness helps the survivor to be released from the emotional bondage of the offense-forgiveness is the step from survivor to warrior.

What to Expect

Some of your group members may have intense feelings at the very thought of forgiving. They may feel anything from fear to rage. To prematurely push members to forgive, before they can process the feelings of fear, shame, and anger, is dangerous. Remind yourself that we forgive because it honors Christ and because it benefits us whether or not our forgiving has any affect on the persons who abused us.

Sexual abuse is a particularly difficult offense to forgive. We need to understand that forgiveness does not justify the people who committed the offense nor give them power to hurt us again. Ultimately, forgiveness releases us from any control perpetrators have over us. Once we assign the responsibility of the offense to the people who committed the offense, then we can choose to forgive them. Before we can assign appropriate responsibility to the offenders, any forgiveness is superficial and harmful.

Skill Development

Evaluate your group for these behaviors.

- Superficial forgiveness: Watch for group members who move to forgiveness without having expressed their hurt, fear, and anger toward the perpetrator. Gently confront them with the need to feel the negative emotions. Use Jesus as an example. He felt hurt, angry and disappointed at the disciples for falling asleep when He asked them to pray.

Before the Session

O Read and complete the learning activities in unit 10 of the member's book.
O Have a flip chart and markers available for use during the session.
O Prepare Scripture/Affirmation cards for unit 11.
O Provide several boxes of tissues.
O Prepare posters of the Parts of Forgiveness, and the Paradox of Forgiveness (see examples below).

The Parts of Forgiveness:
- Make a list of all the effects of the abuse on your life (abuse, abandonment, loss of innocence, etc.).
- Now take each item on your list and forgive the person who injured you and anyone else involved. Ask God to help you to let go of the need to carry the offense.
- Forgive yourself for any survival behaviors that contradicted your values and beliefs.
- Make a list of the behaviors you have developed in order to survive the effects of the abuse (over-reacting, control, perfectionism).
- Now take each item and ask God to restore your awareness of His love to you in place of the feelings of hurt and despair and to help you forgive yourself for these behaviors and the consequences they produce in relationships. Ask God to replace with His love what had been taken from you.

The Paradox of Forgiveness
- You cannot genuinely forgive until you acknowledge the full scope and impact of the offense.
- You cannot forgive and deny the offense at the same time.
- You cannot forgive someone else for an offense and carry responsibility for that same offense yourself.
- You cannot carry shame for an offense yourself and at the same time forgive someone else for it.

During the Session

Arrival-Greet everyone by name. Start on time.

Checking In-
- Ask someone to read the Welcome Statement.

- Ask for a volunteer to share their progress on the assignment given in Group Session 9 about relinquishing control.
- Ask for any other comments or questions on last week's session.

Use the following material from unit 10 to give a mini-lecture on the real meaning of forgiveness. Emphasize that-
- Forgiveness does not mean the abuse was okay!
- Forgiveness does not mean the person has permission to hurt you again!
- Forgiveness does not mean the offense was not great!
- Forgiveness does not depend on the abuser saying he or she is sorry!
- Forgiveness does not mean that the offense was not deliberate or repeated!

Ask members to respond to the following statements from the unit.
- *"Forgiveness is choosing to send away the hurt, the anger, the bitterness, the sadness, and, most important, the abuse."*
- *"My unforgiveness holds me in bondage to the pain of the abuse."*
- *"My forgiving the abuser affects my responses and relationship to him, but the person who committed the abuse is not wholly forgiven unless he goes before God and seeks God's forgiveness. God is the One who atoned for sin. God is the One, and the only One, who pardons the sin of sexual abuse."*

Ask: *What is the difference between rationalization and forgiveness?"* (page 169-170).

Place two tear sheets on the wall. Label the first, "Reasons not to forgive my abuser." Label the other, "Reasons to forgive my abuser." Ask your group members to write as many reasons as they can think of on the sheets. Tell them not to worry if they write some of the same answers. When they have finished, review the sheets using the material from the text and other sources to discuss the importance of forgiveness in recovery.

Be sure that you do not treat forgiveness as a spiritualized form of denial by simply ignoring feelings. Remind your group members that forgiving is a process.

Display your poster on the "Paradox of Forgiveness."
- Discuss the principles on the poster.
- Many of your group members may have never thought about forgiveness in this manner. Allow

plenty of time for them to ask questions and respond to these ideas.
- Ask your group to share how their feelings about forgiveness may have changed based on these ideas.

Remind your group that the process of forgiving is outlined in the member's book. Display and discuss the "Parts of Forgiveness" poster you made prior to the session.

Invite your group members to spend time praying about what they should do about the issues of forgiveness. Remember to reinforce that forgiveness is not denial of the offense.

Quote your memory verse together.
Forgive as the Lord forgave you.
-Colossians 3:13

Quote your unit affirmation together.
Because God has forgiven me,
I can forgive others.

Close with a circle of prayer. End with the "Serenity Prayer."

After the Session

O Pray for each member specifically. Pray for group members with special needs.
O Call each group member. Encourage him or her in the study of the appropriate materials for the next session.
O Use your copy of "Evaluating Each Session." If you have an apprentice, fill in and discuss this worksheet with him or her.
O Discuss with your supervisor or your apprentice the dynamics of the group process.
O Read "Before the Session" for Group Session 11, and carefully complete all the activities in the member's book for unit 11 if you are ready to move to that unit. If you are using a multiple sessions per unit format, review the materials for Group Session 10 to prepare for your next group.

Confronting the Perpetrator

Session Goal: Group members will-
- learn the characteristics common to those who commit sexual abuse;
- learn how to confront the abuser in a healthy way;
- evaluate their own needs and desires about confrontation of their abuser.

You will not advise any group member to confront. You will encourage each member to make the decision to confront or not to confront based on his or her own personal safety, needs, and expectations.

What to Expect

Expect group members to feel much fear and anger as they approach the issue of confrontation. Group members will express many different reasons for not wanting to confront.

Group members tend to fear simulated confrontations almost as much as face-to-face confrontations, because they are really confronting themselves. Confrontations really are about the survivors' confronting their own fear-of their feelings toward the person who abused them.

Skill Development

As you prepare for this session, work on sharpening the following skills.
- Integrate biblical and psychological truth. Scripture includes many examples of God's expressing emotions such as compassion, grief, anger, and joy (see Nehemiah 9:17, John 15:11, Ephesians 4:30). God created us in His image with the capacity to feel deeply. One of the consequences of abuse is that we suppress our God-given capacity to feel. Affirm group members for their capacity to feel intensely about the issue of confrontation.

- Be willing to accept group members where they are. Model acceptance to your group members. Members will have their own individual reasons for their choices about confrontation. Support them where they are on their journey. Trust the Holy Spirit to guide them.

Before the Session

O Read and complete the learning activities in unit 11 of the member's book.
O Have a flip chart and markers available for use during the session.
O Prepare Scripture/Affirmation cards for unit 12.
O Provide several boxes of tissues.
O Make two tear sheets. Label one "Judas" and the other one "The Prodigal Son."
O Provide one three-by-five-inch card for each group member.

During the Session

Arrival-
- Greet each member by name.
- Give everyone a three-by-five-inch card as they arrive.
- Start on time.

Checking In-
- Ask someone to read the Welcome Statement.
- Ask for any comments or questions on last week's session.
- Ask if anyone has an incident they would like to read.

Share Time-
As you begin this session with your group, keep in mind that confronting the abuser directly is not essential to recovery. The survivor does not have to confront. A confrontation done in the right way, with the right motives, and with adequate support and preparation can be a very powerful and meaningful experience; however, it can also be overwhelming and a great disappointment. A confrontation is risky, and the survivor must be prepared for any response the abuser might give.

Breaking the silence of the abuse does not mean confronting the person who committed the abuse. It means talking to supportive people. It means sharing the story. It may or may not involve a confrontation with the perpetrator. The goal of this unit is to help the survivor emotionally confront the issues connected to the abuse. Do not in any way advise or coerce a group member to confront a perpetrator. Be careful about praising and affirming group members who have confronted over those who have chosen not to. Encourage your group members to discuss the issue of confrontation with their counselors and to act in their own best interest.

Use the material from lesson 1 to prepare a mini-lecture on mixed feelings about the person who committed the abuse.

- Ask your group members to write on the three-by-five-inch card what they feel about the person(s) who abused them. Encourage them to write all the feelings they can identify, even conflicting feelings.
- Collect the cards.
- Using the cards, write the feelings on a tear sheet.
- Discuss these feelings with your group.

The cards will allow some distance for those members who may be uncomfortable if they have positive feelings toward the person. After they see that others have the same feelings, they will be more comfortable talking about them.

In lesson 2 the group members were asked to underline characteristics similar to those of their abusers (page 184-185).

- Ask them to share those characteristics with the group.
- As members share, ask them what these characteristics indicate to them about the person who abused them.

Refer your group to the true/false questions in lesson 2 (page 187). Read each question and ask for a response. It will be good for your group to hear these out loud and to respond with a resounding "True" or "False." Encourage the free expression of feelings.

Display the two tear sheets labeled "Judas" and "The Prodigal Son." Brainstorm with your group the difference between the attitudes of these two people. Use the material from page 188 to help guide your group through this comparison.

Use the material in lesson 3 to give a mini-lecture on confrontations. Explain both direct confrontations and simulated confrontations. Be sure to talk about healthy versus unhealthy motives and expectations.

Ask for any questions or feelings about confronting the abuser. Guide the sharing time in a positive direction, making sure that you do not allow group members to move into advising one another.

Refer to lesson 4 on reconciliation. Ask for responses to the exercises on page 194.

- An example of wisdom might be members making wise choices that protect themselves from being abused again.
- Their behavior toward their abusers can be innocent even in the midt of anger and confrontation.
- They can maintain their own integrity while breaking the silence and asserting authority over their own lives.

Use the material on pages 194-198 to discuss the types of responses one might expect from a perpetrator. The three categories are *remorse, denial,* or *rationalization.*

- Write these on a tear sheet.
- Listen for feelings as group members share.

Ask group members to respond to the questions about preparation for confrontation (page 199). Remind your group members that they have already "broken the silence" by telling their story. Encourage them to address the issue of confrontation at their own pace. End this session with encouragement and support for each member, whatever their stage of recovery.

Quote your memory verse together.
When I kept silent, my bones wasted away through my groaning all day long.
-Psalm 32:3

Quote your unit affirmation together.
I can speak the truth. I can be free!

Close with a circle of prayer. End with the "Serenity Prayer."

After the Session

O Pray for each member specifically. Pray for group members with special needs.

O Call each group member. Encourage him or her in the study of the appropriate materials for the next session.

O Use your copy of "Evaluating Each Session." If you have an apprentice, fill in and discuss this worksheet with him or her.

O Discuss with your supervisor or your apprentice the dynamics of the group process.

O Read "Before the Session" for Group Session 12 and carefully complete all the activities in the member's book for unit 12 if you are ready to move to that unit. If you are using a multiple sessions per unit format, review the materials for Group Session 11 to prepare for your next group.

Intimacy in Relationship

Session Goal: Group members will-
- define intimacy;
- discover barriers that make it difficult for them to move toward genuine intimacy;
- recognize reactions in their lives that may be related to their unmet need for healthy intimacy.

What to Expect

Expect your group members to feel a sense of accomplishment. They each have faced at some level what probably is the most difficult challenge of their entire lives. Encourage your members to affirm their progress and the progress of other group members. Also expect your members to express some sadness. To say good-bye to a group is difficult. Even if some of your members will return for a repeat session, the new group will be different as it reforms with new members. Some of your members will experience fear of losing what they have gained. Help them to realize that grief is a normal response to the change but that they will not lose the growth they have experienced.

Before the Session

O Complete the learning activities in unit 12.
O Have a flip chart and markers available.
O Prepare a poster which shows a continuum between isolation and enmeshment.

Tendency to-
isolate .... enmesh

O Provide a three-by-five-inch card for each group-member.

During the Session

Arrival-Greet everyone by name. Start on time.

Checking In-
- Ask someone to read the Welcome Statement.
- Ask for any comments on last week's session.

Share Time-
In this session you will explore the difficulty sexual abuse survivors have with the issue of intimacy. The dysfunctional family relationships and the feelings of betrayal, lack of trust, and the other fears experienced by the survivor create potential barriers to achieving intimacy.

Use the material from page 203 to help your group begin to focus on the need for boundaries and balance in intimate relationships. Share some of the ways you have used to cope with both the need for intimacy and the fear of intimacy. Invite members to share their responses to the learning activity on page 203.

Share your tendency in relationships (page 204). If your tendency is changing through recovery, discuss that change. Invite members to share their relationship tendencies.

Read your definition of *intimacy* (page 207). Invite members to share their definitions of intimacy.
- Brainstorm with your group. Ask someone to record on a tear sheet their responses to the following sentence completions:

    IntimaClJ is_____

    Intimacy does not mean_____

On a tear sheet, list the three factors that can affect a person's ability to express intimacy-
- *The trauma of the abuse*
- *Your relationship to the abuser*
- *The rules and roles in your family system*

Share from pages 203-204 to introduce the poster you prepared prior to the session. Remind your group of the tendency to either shut ourselves off from others or to smother others in our relationships. Ask them to share where they would place themselves on this continuum between isolation and enmeshment.

Ask your group members to share their responses to the learning activities on page 205.
- *What do you believe to be the greatest barriers to your ability to experience intimacy?*
- Ask your group members to share the pictures they

drew that symbolize their struggle with intimacy. What does the picture mean to them?
- Ask your group members to share what it would mean to be intimate with God.
- Ask: *What would it mean to be intimate with your spouse?*

Encourage your group members to continue to work on this issue. Remind them that experiencing intimacy is a strong indication that they are on their way to recovery. Intimacy means trusting, being vulnerable, and risking conflict-things that are difficult for someone who has been severely hurt.

Use the material in lesson 3 to give a mini-lecture on members' loving themselves enough to take care of themselves. Tell your group that one way they can love themselves is to work on their codependency symptoms that result from the abuse. Explain that work in *Shelter* will probably give them a greater capacity to let go of the dysfunctional ways they have attempted to get their intimacy needs met.

Share that the need for intimacy is a God-given need. God said "It is not good for man (humanity) to be alone." Say: *It is especially sad that sexual abuse impacts the most intimate of our relationships-those with whom we want to be romantic.* Talk about the importance of the restoration of clean, healthy feelings about sex and sexuality. Ask members to write on the three-by-five-inch card the attitudes and behaviors they marked with an asterisk on page 219.
- Gather the cards and write the responses on a tear sheet.
- Invite your group members to ask questions or share feelings about the list.
- If members are reluctant to share feelings, ask them to share their responses to the first two learning activities on page 220.

Explain that recovery from sexual abuse is part of the larger discipleship process. Discipleship means growing in Christlikeness. *Shelter from the Storm* ends with some possible ways to continue to grow in our recovery journey and in our discipleship journey.
- Ask group members to share what goals they have for their continued growth in recovery and discipleship.
- Give them plenty of time to support and encourage each other.
- If you are doing the 6-month or 12-month plan, you may want to devote your last session to goals and closure.

Ask each group member to sit in the center of the circle.
- Ask the other members to affirm them for their work and maybe how this person has been helpful to them.
- Ask the group member to read his/her goals.
- Pray for that member.

Repeat your memory verse together.

But If we walk in the light, as he is in the light, we have fellowship one with another, and the blood of Jesus, His Son purifies us from all sin.
– 1 John 1:7

Repeat your unit affirmation together.

I am loved so I can risk loving you.

Read all of your affirmations together (page 213).

Read the following together.

May our Lord Jesus Christ take hold of your right hand and subdue nations before you. May he strip of their armor those that would stand in your way. May he open doors before you so that the gates would not be shut. I pray that Jesus would go before you and level the mountains, break down any gates of bronze or bars of iron. May he indeed give you the treasures in the darkness and the riches that are stored in secret places. I pray that you would know without a doubt that it is the Lord God of Israel who has called you by name.

I pray that you would have the wings of a dove! That you would have the freedom to fly away from the discouragement and pain and to be at rest. That you would allow Jesus to be your place of shelter, far from the tempest and storm.
-Based on Isaiah 45:1-3, Psalm 55:6-8

Close with a circle of prayer. End with the "Serenity Prayer."

After the Session

O Use your copy of "Evaluating Each Session." If you have an apprentice, fill in and discuss this worksheet with him or her.

O Discuss with your supervisor or your apprentice the dynamics of the group process. Decide about changes for your next series of sessions.

O Call each group member, evaluate need and potential for repeat sessions.

Support Group Guidelines

- The purpose of this group is to provide a safe environment where mutual support and accountability can strengthen the members.
- We charge no fees for the group. You may be asked to purchase books and materials.
- This is not a therapy group. The facilitator's role is to guide the sharing process.
- The facilitator does not give specific advice or direction about decisions members need to make, but the facilitator enlists the resources of the group to assist members to make wise decisions.
- The group is not a substitute for professional individual or group therapy. If a person's needs are not met in the group, the person will be referred to a competent professional.
- To encourage members to address their issues in the group setting, the facilitator is not available for one-on-one counseling with group members.
- The content and style of this group will be guided by Christian principles.
- Participation in the group is voluntary.

Confidentiality

Confidentiality is a hallmark of a safe group; however, the facilitator is required by law to report certain issues to appropriate authorities. These include:
- a group member who threatens to do harm to self or others.
- a group member who is or has been involved in harm to a child or elderly person.

If a group member learns of these threats or behaviors, the facilitator should be informed immediately.

Group Rules:

1. Whatever is said in the group stays in the group.
2. Use "I" messages, not "you" messages.
3. Do not give advice unless it is requested.
4. You do not have to talk if you do not want to.
5. Do not use humor to cover your pain.

I understand the purpose, nature, and limitations of this group. I agree to abide by the rules of the group and to follow the procedures of the group.

Signed : ---

Date:_____

Make two copies: one for the group member, the other for the facilitator's records.

Welcome Statement

Welcome to *Shelter from the Storm*. We call this group *Shelter from the Storm* because we acknowledge that sexual abuse is a storm from which we need the shelter of hope and encouragement. We all need support as we face our emotions, pain, and tears. We believe that Jesus is the ultimate shelter from the storm. The Bible says to "bear one another's burdens and thus fulfill the law of Christ" (Galatians 6:2, NASB). We will provide shelter for each other as we share and support one another. We know that we can find peace in the midst of the worst of storms.

In *Shelter* we define sexual abuse as any behavior of a sexual nature-physical, verbal, or visual-imposed on an adult or on a child by another person. Some of us have been abused by members of our immediate or extended families, by trusted family friends, and other people in whom we have placed our trust and confidence. Some of us have been abused by a stranger. Regardless of the circumstances surrounding the abuse we recognize that we have been severely affected. The abuse has damaged our lives whether it occurred once or many times. We have been affected regardless of our response at the time of the abuse.

We are different in many ways, but because of our abuse, we share many traits. We share a common trauma. The trauma of sexual abuse impacted our lives contradicting our values, beliefs, self-image, and the reality of our world. As a result of those contradictions most of us struggle with losses such as self-esteem, safety, security, self-worth, and trust. Each of us developed thoughts, attitudes, and behaviors that allowed us to survive the abuse. We sometimes tried to fill our need for value and worth through dependencies on people, food, sex, and/or chemicals.

We will learn in this group that we did not imagine, nor were we responsible for, our abuse. Here we learn again to trust, to share, and to love. We regain our dignity. Most of us feel the pain of being different, and of being abandoned and betrayed. Because of our common background, we can share our pain. We can learn together how to talk about and resolve the trauma of sexual abuse. We can be together and share our story. We can trust one another to keep confidential what is said in our group. We need one another. We have been alone too long. Here, together, we can learn, one day at a time, that we truly are survivors. Because we can find Shelter from the Storm we can overcome the effects of sexual abuse and thrive in the abundant life God intended for us.

Scripture/ Affirmation Cards

Unitt

I said, "Oh, that I had the wings of a dove! I would fly away and be at rest- I would flee far away and stay in the desert; I would hurry to my place of shelter, far from the tempest and storm."

-Psalm 55:6-8

I can find hope and healing.

Unit2

Who satisfies your years with good things, so that your youth is renewed like the eagle.

-Psalm 103:5, NASB

I oo.ccept Go.:A.'s love oo.\\.:A. ki\\.:A.\\ess towoo.v-.:A.   Me.

Unit3

You will know the truth, and the truth will set you free.

-John 8:32

The tvv.H" will set Me -Pvee!

Unit4

I will turn the darkness into light before them and make the rough places smooth. These are the things I will do; I will not forsake them.

-Isaiah 42:16

I oo.IM wov-tlr.y to Y.oo.ve Go.:A. leoo.J.. IMe 0\\\J.. COIM.Pov-t IMe.

Unit 5

You will forget the shame of your youth.

-Isaiah 54:4

I am clean.

Unit6

There is now no condemnation for those who are in Christ Jesus.

-Romans 8:1

I am wonderfully made.

Unit7

Be angry, and yet do not sin.

-Ephesians 4:26, NASB

I 1.'\oo.ve pev- Missio\\ to .Peel MY oo.\\Bev oo. J.. 1.'\v.v-t.

UnitS

Even though I walk through the valley of the shadow of death, I will fear no evil, for you are with me; your rod and staff, they comfort me.

-Psalm 23:4

In Christ I am never alone.

Unit9

May the God of hope fill you with all joy and peace as you trust in him, so that you may overflow with hope by the power of the Holy Spirit.

-Romans 15:13

I can trust myself and others.

Unit 10

Forgive as the Lord forgave you.

-Colossians 3:13

Becoo.v.se Go.:A. 1.'\oo.s .Pov-BiVe\\ Me, I coo.\\ .Pov-Bive otlr.evs.

Unit 11

When I kept silent, my bones wasted away through my groaning all day long.

-Psalm 32:3

I coo. speoo. tlr.e tvv.tk I coo.\\ e .Pvee!

Unit 12

But If we walk in the light, as he is in the light, we have fellowship one with another, and the blood of Jesus, His Son purifies us from all sin.

-1 John 1:7

I oo.IM love.:A., so I coo.\\ vis lovi\\8 yov..

You have permission to reproduce this page for your *Shelter from the Storm* group. We recommend reproducing this page onto a heavier card stock so your group members may carry each card with them.

How to Give Support

Your friend or family member will be participating in a support group called *Shelter from the Storm*. This group is for survivors of sexual abuse. Because the issues involved in this process are so difficult, members must build a support network. You are being asked to be a support person while your friend is in the group. The information in this packet will help you to understand about the role of a support person. After you read it carefully, you can decide if you are willing to help in this significant way. Your friend or family member has taken a major step by sharing this information with you. Please honor his or her trust by maintaining confidentiality.

Supporting doesn't mean taking care of or being responsible for this person. When you are in doubt, you can ask your friend what kind of support they need. Your friend will need to know that you care and that you will listen without giving advice. You are not responsible to fix your friend or to remove the pain. You will help by supporting as your friend learns to deal with the pain and with the results of the abuse. Because support is so often misunderstood, this information has been prepared to help you and the person you are supporting understand your role.

Survivors of sexual abuse are dealing with an injury that cannot be seen. Recovery takes time. If they had broken arms or legs as a result of a car accident, friends would rush in to help. Most people, even casual acquaintances, would be willing supporters during the victim's healing process. But if recovery were to take a long, long time, even a willing participant might grow weary. A real problem for you will be that you can't see the brokenness of your friend or family member's heart. The brokenness of a bone is evident, by x-ray if not by outward appearance. Your friend's heart may be truly shattered, but unfortunately, there is no x-ray to show friends. This person will have to help you understand that the pain is real even though you can't see it.

What Not to Say

You will want to help your friend-to stop the pain or to provide answers. In a desire to help, many caring people cause additional injury. The list below contains "The Don'ts." The 15 statements in this list are all words that family members, close friends, or well-meaning Christians might say to a sexual abuse survivor. These words and phrases are not helpful.

Don't say to survivors-
- "Why are you making such a big deal of this? You were very young at the time it happened."
- "What did you do to make this happen?"
- "You're the problem. You're just using this as an excuse to get your way."
- "Why didn't you stop it from happening?"
- "You mean you didn't tell anybody when it happened? So why tell now?"
- "Why can't you just forget it?"
- "You should just forgive and forget. God won't be there for you unless you forgive."
- "I don't believe you were ever abused."
- "What is past is past. Let's just not bring it up again."
- "Just pray about it. God will take care of it."
- "Why can't you just hurry up and get over this?"
- "I'm so sick of hearing about your needs. What about my needs?"
- "You are just feeling sorry for yourself."
- "Can't you just let go of it? Nothing is happening to you now."
- "It is a sin to think about this. God says to focus on what is good."
- "The Bible says to forget the past and to press on to the future."

The Requirements of Giving

The most important gift you can give your recovering friend is the time to heal. Allow your friend to feel angry or sad. Do not think that you are responsible to fix the problem. You will be supporting your friend as he or she learns to deal with responsibility and to trust others appropriately. Your greatest service will be to listen and to daily pray for your friend.

For most survivors, one of the most difficult struggles of recovery will be to rely on others. At times you may be required to be giving more than you can give. Sometimes you may feel like you are incapable of giving.

Survivors need friends, family, other survivors, and their relationship with Christ in order to overcome the trauma of abuse. Sometimes those who care don't know how to support. Below is a list of attitudes and behaviors helpful to the abuse survivor. You may want to read them many times as you support the friend or family member that has shared this packet with you and requested your support.

The Do's
Friends and family can be helpful by standing ready to give-

- Support
- Acceptance
  - Love
  - Time
- Understanding
- Interest
- Forgiveness
  - Help

- Belief
- Prayer support
- Encouragement
- Hope
- Honor
- Trust
- Validation

Survivors of sexual abuse need open, honest, accepting communication. When you do not know what to say or to do, say to your friend, "I don't know what to say or do. What do you need from me?" Frequently the answer will be that you just need to listen and support.

Recovery is a journey that only the recovering person can make. Support groups use the slogan: "Only you can do it, but you can't do it alone." You are not being asked to go on the journey. You are being asked to be supportive of your friend as he or she goes on the journey.

As your friend or family member works through recovery, you also will be affected. Your friend is using a workbook called *Shelter from the Storm* and attending a support group of the same name. LifeWay Press also supplies a workbook for those who have a loved one in recovery. It is called *Family and Friends: Helping the Person You Care About in Recovery.* Many churches also offer a group for family members and friends. This group and workbook can help you better to understand what your friend is experiencing, what goes on in a support group, and how better to help him or her. To learn more about *Family and Friends,* ask your friend, the facilitator of the *Shelter from the Storm* group, or your local church small-group coordinator. You may call 1-800-458-2772 to order. Ask for item number 7200-26.

The Goals of the Recovery Process

You may well wonder, "What is the point of recovery?" "What is my friend trying to achieve?" The following list contains the indications of recovery. These attitudes and actions are sign posts along the way. People do recover from the trauma of sexual abuse. The recovery may be slow but with support it does happen. The process is somewhat different for each survivor, but there are indications that recovery is happening. Look for the following in your survivor and affirm him or her for these things.

The survivor will-
- be willing to face the abuse and acknowledge the hurt and the pain.
- recognize that he/she was a victim even though he/she may have experienced physical arousal during the abuse.
- understand that the abuse was a violation.
- have an increased awareness of personal value and worth.
- list significant others whom he/she can trust.
- share thoughts and feelings about the abuse to others.
- recognize relationship tendencies that avoid honesty and intimacy
- overcome feelings of shame and false guilt.

Now that you have read this description of the process, what questions do you have? Write below your questions or issues you need to discuss with your friend who has asked for your support.

_____

_____

_____

_____

_____

_____

_____

_____

_____

Thank you for considering being a support-person. Please remember the most important thing you can do for your friend or family member is to pray for them as they go through the recovery process. We ask that you also pray for yourself. Please allow God to guide you as you make the decision to support this person.

Cycle of False Beliefs

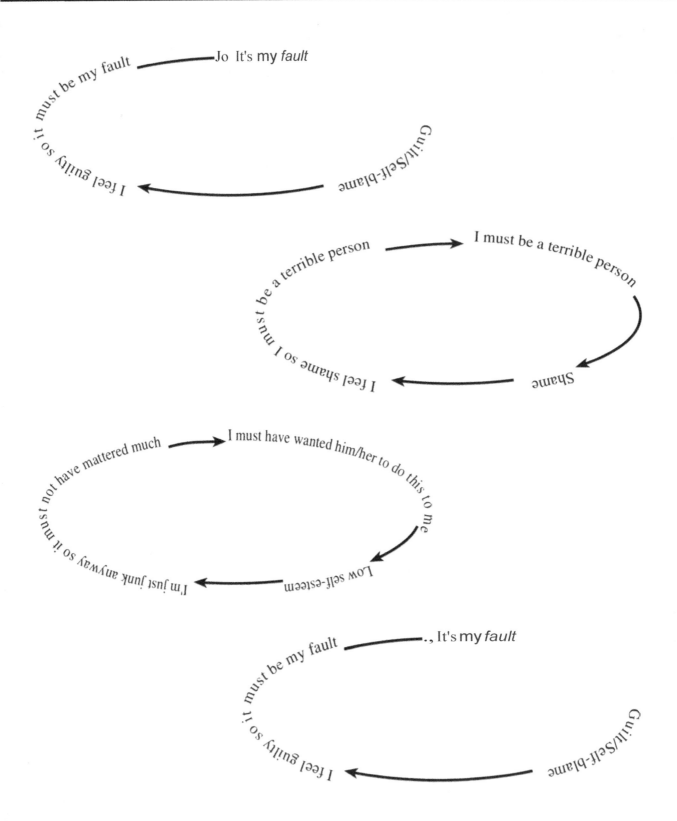

Feeling Facts

1. Feelings are neither right nor wrong-only actions can be judged that way.

2. Feelings are affected by how we think-negative thoughts produce negative feelings.

3. Feelings are often mixed-rarely do you experience one feeling at a time.

4. Feelings can be expressed in different ways-there is no one right way, each person has his/her own style.

5. Feelings are sometimes easier to handle if you put a picture or image to them. For example state the feeling (fear) then the picture, "I feel like a little kid lost in a big store." or (anger) "I feel like a red monster ready to destroy everything."

6. Strong feelings need to be experienced in doses-enough to feel but not to be overwhelmed.

7. Feelings do not lose their intensity by being buried, even for a long time. They must be worked through to lose their punch.

MY PLAN FOR MANAGING CRISIS

I must learn to ask for help and be willing to accept help when it is offered. When I feel overwhelmed with my emotions, anxiety, depression, or suicidal thoughts I will contact the following individual(s):

I will call_____at_____.

If that person is not available, I will call_____at_____as backup.

I may also call my pastor at_____or my counselor at_____

Others who have agreed to be a support for me-

_____   _____

_____   _____

Life is worth living because . . .

_____

_____

_____

MY PLAN FOR MANAGING CRISIS

I must learn to ask for help and be willing to accept help when it is offered. When I feel overwhelmed with my emotions, anxiety, depression, or suicidal thoughts I will contact the following individual(s):

I will call _____ at_____

If that person is not available, I will call_____at_____as backup.

I may also call my pastor at_____or my counselor at_____

Others who have agreed to be a support for me-

_____   _____

_____   _____

Life is worth living because . . .

_____

_____

_____

Resources

The Search For Significance
McGee, Robert S., Houston. Word Publishing: 1986. Teaching who you are in Christ, this seminal book, which has sold 3 million copies, is the cornerstone for recovery from all addictions.

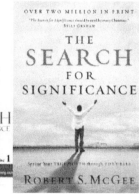

Shelter From the Storm
Littlefield, Cynthia Kubetin with James Mallory, M.D. Houston. Word Publishing. 1993. In a powerful way, this book tells the story of how many people survived the trauma of sexual abuse, reaching full recovery.

Father Hunger
McGee, Robert S. Houston. Word Publishing: 1993. This book is for people who didn't receive the quality of love they needed, required or deserved from their fathers, when they were small children.

The Search For Freedom
McGee, Robert S., West Palm Beach. Word Publishing: 1993. This book uncovers the strongholds we create to survive dysfunctional homes, including how to dismantle them.

The Search For Peace
McGee, Robert S., West Palm Beach. Word Publishing: 1993. True forgiveness is really God's forgiveness, which is complete and not what most people consider it to be.

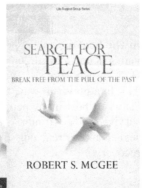

Conquering Chemical Dependency

McGee, Robert S. and Dale W. McClesky. Rapha Publishing and Word Publishing. Houston: 1994. Biblically based and clinically tested, this is a proven 12-step approach, providing significant aid for addicted people. It will help them make a complete recovery from chemical addiction.

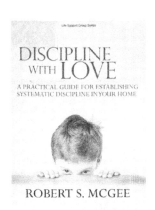

Discipline With Love

McGee, Robert S. and Dale W. McClesky. McGee Publishing. West Palm Beach: 2003. This is a practical guide for establishing systematic discipline in your home.

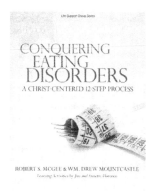

Conquering Eating Disorders

McGee, Robert S. and William Drew Mountcastle. Houston. Word Publishing: 1993. This effective program tackles the compulsive-addictive patterns that cause a person to use food to gain control as a medication for painful feelings.

Breaking the Cycle of Hurtful Family Relationships

McGee, Robert S. with Pat Springle and Jim Craddock. West Palm Beach. Robert S McGee Publishing: 1986. This insightful book will help you understand how your parents shaped the way you feel about yourself, about how you relate to others, and also about how you formed your ideas about God.

Conquering Codependency

Springle, Pat. Houston. Rapha Publishing and Word Publishing: 1993. This 12 Step Program helps people recognize the painful problems stemming from codependency, which is the compulsion to fix everyone and everything. It includes ways for the person to achieve freedom from codependency.

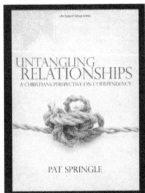

Untangling Relationships

Springle, Pat. Houston. Rapha Publishing: 1993. This is a time-tested program that is effective in helping a person identify the painful effects of codependency—the compulsion to help fix everyone and everything.

Hi My Name Is Jack

Watts, Jack. New York. Simon & Schuster: 2011. Jack's story is true and authentic. It's about a guy who had no alternative but to trust God. His story is not sappy or religious, but gut-wrenchingly honest.

Real Prayers For Real People With Real Problems

Watts, Jack. Nashville. Dunham Books: 2012. Many have suffered emotional and mental abuse, plunging them into a revolving door of self-destructive behavior, which spirals out of control. For those in these desperate situations, here are fifty-two genuine and authentic prayers that will help them reconnect with a loving and merciful God.

Recovering From Religious Abuse: 11 Steps to Spiritual Freedom

Watts, Jack. New York. Simon & Schuster: 2011. When Christians are used, abused and discarded by trusted religious leaders, they discard Christianity and God. This 11-step program can help these 40 million people reestablish an intimate relationship with the Lord.

We Believe: 30 Days to Understanding Our Heritage

Watts, Jack. Nashville. Dunham Books: 2012. By spending just ten minutes a day for one month, the reader can understand the values that made America exceptional. Based on the original documents, anybody can come to understand our great traditions.

The Search for Reality

As followers of Christ, we have been promised the abundant life, but most of us don't experience it. Actually, our lives are not much different than our non-Christian friends. In fact, statistically there is no difference.

Instead of making you feel guilty about this, The Search for Reality addresses the problem head-on, providing answers that will revolutionize your life. Most Christian books over promise and under deliver—but not The Search for Reality. The pages of this book contain the material necessary for you to become the person God created you to be. Your life will fundamentally change and you exhibit the Christ-like qualities of love, joy, peace, patience, kindness, goodness, faithfulness, gentleness, and self-control. If this is what you want for your life, but it has always eluded you, The Search for Reality is definitely for you.

Made in the USA
Monee, IL
30 September 2023